De GUSTIBUS PRESENTS
THE GREAT COOKS' COOKBOOKS

French Cooking
FOR THE HOME

DE GUSTIBUS PRESENTS
THE GREAT COOKS' COOKBOOKS

French Cooking

FOR THE HOME

ARLENE FELTMAN-SAILHAC

PHOTOGRAPHS BY TOM ECKERLE

DESIGN BY MARTIN LUBIN

BLACK DOG & LEVENTHAL

NEW YORK

Published by

Black Dog & Leventhal Publishers, Inc.
151 West 19th Street
New York, NY 10011

Distributed by

Workman Publishing Company
708 Broadway
New York, NY 10003

Manufactured in Hong Kong

ISBN: 1-884822-15-0

h g f e d c b a

Daniel Boulud's recipes adapted from *Easy Cooking with Daniel Boulud* by Daniel Boulud. Copyright © 1993 by Daniel Boulud. Adapted by permission of Random House, Inc., New York.

Sweet Green Tomato Pie adapted from Tomato Tourte in *Antoine Bouterin's Desserts from Le Périgord* with Ruth Gardner. Copyright © 1989 by Antoine Bouterin. Used by permission of G.P. Putnam's Sons, New York.

Julia Child's recipes are reprinted by permission of Julia Child. Artichoke Bottoms Filled with Poached Oysters appears in *Julia Child: The Way to Cook* by Julia Child. Copyright © 1989 by Julia Child. Published by Alfred A. Knopf, New York.

Fillet of Beef with Horseradish Sauce from *Cuisine Rapide* by Pierre Franey and Bryan Miller. Copyright © 1989 by Pierre Franey and Bryan Miller. Adapted by permission of Times Books, a division of Random House, Inc., New York.

Lettuce Soup; Scallopine of Turkey Breast with Morel and Cognac Sauce; and Fricassee of Turkey and Brown Rice adapted from *Cuisine Economique* by Jacques Pépin. Copyright © 1992 by Jacques Pépin. By permission of William Morrow & Company, Inc., New York.

Apple Bonne Femme adapted from *Everyday Cooking with Jacques Pépin* by Jacques Pépin. Copyright © 1982 by Jacques Pépin. By permission of Harper & Row, New York.

Napoléon of Roquefort and Boursin; and Wild Mushroom Gateau from *Simple Cuisine: The Easy, New Approach to Four-Star Cooking* by Jean-Georges Vongerichten. Copyright © 1990 by Jean-Georges Vongerichten. Used by permission of Prentice Hall Press / A Division of Simon & Schuster, New York.

DEDICATION

I dedicate this book to my family, which loves to eat:

My parents, Adelaide and Stanley Kessler

My sister, brother-in-law, and niece, Gayle, Stanley, and Amy Miller

My Grandma Berdie, who opened my eyes to food

And to Alain Sailhac and Todd Feltman, the two "men in my life who are my favorite dining partners."

ACKNOWLEDGMENTS

During the fourteen-year existence of De Gustibus at Macy's, many people have given their support and encouragement.

First, my profound thanks to all the wonderful chefs and cooks who have taught at De Gustibus at Macy's. A special thanks to David Bouley, Daniel Boulud, Antoine Bouterin, Julia Child, Christian Delouvrier, Jean-Michel Diot, Pierre Franey, Gray Kunz, Jacques Pépin, Alain Sailhac, André Soltner, Jean-Georges Vongerichten.

Thanks to my priceless assistants who are always there for me in a million ways: Jane Asche, Barbara Bjorn, Pam Carey, Corinne Gherardi, Yonina Jacobs, Nancy Robbins, and Betti Zucker.

Thanks to Barbara Teplitz for all her help and support throughout the years, and to Gertrud Yampierre for holding the office together.

Thanks to Ruth Schwartz for believing in the concept of De Gustibus and helping to orchestrate its initiation at Macy's.

Thanks to everyone at Macy's Herald Square who have supported De Gustibus at Macy's since its inception, with special notice to the Public Relations and Advertising Departments who helped spread the word.

Thanks to J.P. Leventhal and Pamela Horn of Black Dog & Leventhal Publishers for providing the vehicle to put our cooking classes into book form and for being so encouraging.

A special thanks to Jane Asche for her help in the beginning stages of the book.

Thanks to Tom Eckerle for his magical photographs; Ceci Gallini for her impeccable taste and prop design; and Roscoe Betsill, whose food styling really took this project to another level.

Thanks for supplying the exquisite props for the photographs to Pierre Deux, N.Y.C., and Takashimaya, N.Y.C.

Thanks for allowing us to shoot photographs on location in Provence to: Andrée Collisson et Claude De Wolf, Didier Collisson at Le Château des Baumettes; Minouche et François Cance at L'Herbier; Jacques et Doune Hermitte at Le Mas des Gres.

Thanks to Marty Lubin for his wonderful design.

Thanks to Mary Goodbody, Sarah Bush, Judith Sutton, and testers Deborah Callan and Elizabeth Wheeler for making the book "user friendly."

Thanks to my agent Judith Weber for her help and advice.

Special thanks to Judith Choate, who shaped all my words into meaningful prose and never ceased to amaze me with her knowledge of food and her patience and calm, and to Steve Pool for getting these words into the computer with smiles and enthusiasm.

Heartfelt thanks to the entire Kobrand Corporation, purveyors of fine wine, especially Cathleen Burke and Kimberly Charles for opening the door for the marriage of fine wine and great food for the last ten years.

Finally, thanks to all the faithful De Gustibus customers who have made all our classes spring to life.

Contents

Foreword

Fourteen years ago, the popularity of cooking classes was growing all over the United States. While interest was high, New Yorkers could not always fit an ongoing series of classes into their busy schedules. Demonstration classes seemed to me to be the answer and De Gustibus was born. What began as four chefs and an electric frying pan on a stage developed into over 350 chefs and cooking teachers demonstrating their specialties in a professionally equipped kitchen for groups of fervent food-lovers.

When we started De Gustibus in 1980, we had no inkling of the variety of new cuisines that would become an integral part of American cooking. Since then we have discovered New World Cuisine, Florida Cuisine, Light Cooking, Fusion Cooking, Cajun Cooking, Southwest Cooking—you name it! As American and international cuisines have changed and our tastes have broadened, De Gustibus has stayed on the cutting edge of the culinary experience. We have invited teachers, cooks, and chefs to De Gustibus both because of their level of recognition in the food world, and because of challenging, unique, current, and, above all, noteworthy cooking styles.

The goal of the cooking demonstrations at De Gustibus is to make the art of the grand master chefs and cooks accessible and practical for the home kitchen. Each chef leads the way and holds out a helping hand to the home cook. The results depend as much on the cook's wit, self-confidence, and interest as they do on a great recipe. Thus, students, and now readers of this book, can learn to master the recipes of the most sophisticated chefs and cooks.

The reason De Gustibus demonstration classes are so popular is that they allow the novice the opportunity to feel the passion—as well as to see each professional chef's or cook's technique, order, and discipline. By seeing how each chef's personality influences the final product, serious home cooks gain the confidence to trust their own tastes and instincts. New and unfamiliar ingredients, untried techniques, and even a little dazzle all find a place in the amateur's kitchen.

This book introduces some of the best and most popular menus demonstrated throughout the years. Each dish is designed to serve six people, unless otherwise noted. All the menus were prepared in class and I have done little to alter them, other than to test and streamline recipes for the home kitchen. I have also provided each chef's strategy and Kobrand Distributors' wine suggestions with every recipe.

ARLENE FELTMAN-SAILHAC
1995

Introduction

De Gustibus Presents the Great Cooks' Cookbook: French Cooking for the Home is dedicated to the French-trained chefs. It includes recipes that are classic culinary treasures, modern haute cuisine, bistro favorites, and both regional and cosmopolitan in scope. Although each chef is a product of traditional French training, they all have, for the most part, been deeply influenced by the ingredients and techniques of cuisines from all parts of the world now internationally available.

All of the French-trained chefs and cooks are masters of knife skills, which translates to speed in preparation of ingredients. They are constantly wiping and washing their work spaces as they cut and chop and measure. They are captains of taste, sipping after every addition, continually adjusting the flavor. Above all, French-trained chefs and cooks have incredible respect for their ingredients: nothing wasted, every element used.

All of the chefs and cooks we feature love sharing their passion with home cooks. The way they impart their professional knowledge inspires a confidence that we didn't know we had, and with their guidance we do succeed in translating their skills to our own hands and hearts.

Even though their specialty is French cuisine, not all of the chefs and cooks in this book were born in France. In fact, some of them could not be more American. But you would never suspect their heritage when you experience their typical Gallic love and respect for food.

My first encounter with the marvel of a French chef was during the early days of the De Gustibus cooking theater. Jacques Pépin, who was fascinated by *garde manger* at the time—that is, the decorative aspects of dishes—came to teach us about sculpting fruits and vegetables. We had not yet learned of the need for overhead mirrors, microphones, or a complete pantry. Consequently, we had about 80 people stretching their necks and shushing their neighbors as they tried to hear Jacques, and watch him carve a turtle out of a cucumber, a pig out of a lemon, a rabbit out of an olive and so forth. Needless to say, I learned more about what we would have to do to run successful cooking classes than the students learned about *garde manger.*

Mise-en-place tray

The next Francophile in the De Gustibus kitchen was Julia Child. In her confident manner, Julia was not at all put off by her lack of equipment. Arriving with a blow torch to peel her tomatoes, she taught us something about creating great meals with what you have at hand.

When De Gustibus finally moved to the world-famous Macy's and into a proper demonstration kitchen, I had the courage to ask André Soltner, founding owner-chef of New York's four-star French restaurant, Lutèce, to join us. What a revelation he was to all of us. Chef Soltner would have been a star no matter where we were. Standing alone, without sous chef, preparation assistants, or pastry chef, he cooked for 80 people in the most impeccable but relaxed style imaginable.

Along the way, the classes at De Gustibus have experienced French chefs literally "just off the boat," speaking little English but reaching out to us and teaching us through our mutual love of great meals. Perhaps the famous Gallic charm has also had something to do with the warmth our students have felt for our roster of French chefs. I have come to understand the love of good food and I can attest to the veracity of Gallic charm—since I married one of these treasures of France!

STRATEGIES FOR COOKING
FROM OUR GREAT CHEFS AND COOKS

Before beginning to prepare any meal, regardless of how simple or how complicated, take the following steps to heart:

1. Read through the entire menu and its recipes in advance.

2. Complete as many recipes or steps as possible ahead of time, taking care to allow time for defrosting, reheating, bringing to room temperature, or whatever the recipe calls for, before serving.

For each menu we have provided a feature entitled "What You Can Prepare Ahead of Time." This provides time-saving hints for the cook who is preparing the entire menu, or elements of it, and wants to do as much of the preparation before the actual day of the meal as possible. While you may know that many foods taste better fresh, rather than reheated, we have included this list for your convenience, to offer *suggestions*, not *required* do-ahead instructions.

3. Place all the ingredients for a particular recipe on, or in, individual trays, plates, or bowls according to the specific steps in the recipe. Each item should be washed, chopped, measured, separated—or whatever is called for. This organizational technique, known as the *mise en place* (from the French, it literally means "putting into place"), is the most valuable lesson we at De Gustibus have learned from the pros. We strongly urge you to cook this way.

Note that when a recipe calls for a particular ingredient to be cut in a certain size or shape, it matters. The final result is often dependent upon the textures and color, as well as the flavor of the ingredients.

4. Use only the best ingredients available. All good chefs and cooks stress this. Try to find the exact ingredient called for, but if you cannot, substitute as suggested in the recipe or glossary, or use your common sense.

5. Rely on your taste buds. They will not lie!

6. Don't forget to clean up as you work.

Use the following menu suggestions in full, or plan meals around one or two elements from a menu. Educate yourself, and have fun with these impressive French recipes adapted for the home.

The Cooks

DAVID BOULEY
Chef/Owner,
Bouley, New York,
New York

CHRISTIAN DELOUVRIER
Executive Chef, *Les Célébrités,* Essex House Hotel, New York, New York

JACQUES PÉPIN
Cookbook author, teacher, and TV personality, Madison, Connecticut
Dean of Special Programs at *The French Culinary Institute,* New York, New York

DANIEL BOULUD
Chef/Owner,
Daniel Restaurant,
New York, New York

JEAN-MICHEL DIOT
Chef/Owner, *Park Bistro* and *Park Avenue Gourmandise,* New York, New York

ALAIN SAILHAC
Dean of Culinary Arts at *The French Culinary Institute,* New York, New York
Former Executive Chef, *Le Cirque,* New York, New York

ANTOINE BOUTERIN
Executive Chef,
Le Périgord,
New York, New York

PIERRE FRANEY
Chef, cookbook author, and TV personality, New York, New York

ANDRÉ SOLTNER
Executive Chef,
Lutèce, New York,
New York

JULIA CHILD
Grande Dame of French Cooking, cookbook author, and TV personality, Cambridge, Massachusetts

GRAY KUNZ
Executive Chef,
Lespinasse Restaurant,
The St. Regis Hotel,
New York, New York

JEAN-GEORGES VONGERICHTEN
Chef/Owner, *JoJo* and *Vong,* New York, New York

11

Techniques

CUTTING VEGETABLES

Into julienne: Using a small, very sharp knife, a mandoline, or an inexpensive vegetable slicer, cut vegetables into thin, uniform sticks, usually about ¼-inch thick and 1 to 2 inches long. This process is easiest when each vegetable is first cut into uniform pieces. For instance, trim a bell pepper into two or three evenly shaped pieces and then proceed to cut into a julienne.

Into a dice: Trim vegetables into uniform rectangles. Using a very sharp knife, cut into strips ranging in width from ⅛ to ¼ inch, depending upon the size dice you require. Lay the strips together and cut into an even dice by cross cutting into squares ⅛ to ¼ inch across. When dicing bell peppers, it is particularly important to trim all the membranes and ridges so that you have an absolutely smooth rectangle.

Tourner: This French term literally means "to turn." When used to describe the preparation of vegetables, it means to trim them into small, uniform shapes (generally oval or olive-shaped) using a very sharp knife or parer. The vegetable to be turned is usually cut into quarters and then each piece is made uniform by trimming the flesh as you turn it in your fingers. The vegetable should have seven sides. This preparation facilitates the uniform cooking of the vegetables.

CLARIFYING BUTTER

Clarified butter burns less easily than other butter because during the clarifying process, the milk particles are removed. For the same reason it stores longer.

CLARIFIED BUTTER
MAKES ABOUT 3 CUPS

2 pounds unsalted butter, cut into pieces

1 Melt the butter in a medium-sized saucepan over very low heat. Skim off the foam that rises to the top using a ladle, taking care to remove as little of the clear, yellow fat as possible.

2 Let the butter cool slightly and settle. Carefully strain the butter through a fine sieve into a clean, glass container, leaving the milky residue on the bottom of the saucepan. Discard the residue.

3 Cover and refrigerate for up to 2 weeks or freeze for up to 1 month.

ROASTING PEPPERS

Using a fork with a heat-proof handle, hold the chile or pepper close to the flame of a gas stove-top burner without actually placing it in the flame, until the skin puffs and is charred black. Turn as necessary to ensure that the entire pepper is charred. Immediately place the charred chile or pepper in a plastic bag and seal. Allow to steam for about 10 minutes.

Remove the chile or pepper from the bag and pull off the charred skin. Stem and seed. Dice, chop, or purée as required.

If using an electric stove, place the entire pepper in a large, dry, cast-iron skillet over moderately high heat. Slowly cook, turning frequently, until completely charred. Proceed as above.

To roast several peppers at a time, place on a baking sheet under a preheated broiler. Place as close to heat as possible without touching flame. Roast until skin puffs and is charred black. As necessary, turn to char entire chile or pepper. Continue as above to remove skin and prepare chile or pepper for use.

ROASTING GARLIC

You may roast whole heads of garlic (bulbs) or you may cut each head in half, crosswise, or separate each one into individual cloves.

ROASTED GARLIC

1 or more whole garlic heads (bulbs) or 1 or more cloves garlic

1 Preheat the oven to 200 degress F.

2 Lightly wrap the garlic in aluminum foil. Place on a pie plate or small baking sheet. Bake for 1 hour for a whole head, 15 minutes for individual cloves, or until the pulp is very soft. Remove from the oven. Unwrap and allow to cool.

For whole heads: Cut in half crosswise, and working from the closed end, gently push the soft roasted garlic from the skin. Discard the skin.

For individual cloves: Slit the skin using a sharp knife point. Gently push the soft roasted garlic from the skin. Discard the skin.

TOASTING AND SKINNING NUTS

Preheat oven to 400 degrees F. Lay the nuts in a single layer on a baking sheet or pie tin. Using a spray bottle such as those used to mist plants, lightly spray the nuts with cool water. Roast for 5 to 10 minutes, depending on the nut's size and oil content, or until golden. Remember, since nuts have a high oil content, they can burn very quickly. Immediately remove from oven and transfer to a cool plate or tray to cool. If you leave them on the baking sheet, they will continue to cook. If the nuts have skins, immediately spread them on a clean kitchen towel. Let them cool slightly and then wrap them in the towel and rub the nuts back and forth to remove the skins.

If you do not need to toast nuts but want to skin them, put them in boiling water for 1 minute. Drain well. Place in a clean kitchen towel and rub the nuts back and forth to remove the skins.

Pantry Recipes

We supply standard stock recipes for chicken, turkey, and beef, lamb or veal stock used in the recipes. Homemade stock adds a depth of flavor to a dish not possible with canned broth. However, if time is a factor, use canned chicken (or beef) broth, buying those brands that are labeled "low-sodium." Do not use diluted bouillon cubes; they are excessively salty.

CHICKEN OR TURKEY STOCK
MAKES ABOUT 4 CUPS
PREPARATION TIME: ABOUT 40 MINUTES
COOKING TIME: ABOUT 2 HOURS AND 30 MINUTES

2 quarts (8 cups) water
2 chicken carcasses or 5 pounds turkey bones, cut in small pieces
3 onions, chopped
1 carrot, chopped
2 ribs celery, chopped
3 sprigs fresh thyme
3 sprigs fresh parsley
1 bay leaf
1 tablespoon white peppercorns

1 In a large saucepan or stockpot, combine the water and chopped carcasses. Bring to a simmer over medium heat and skim the surface of any foam.

2 Add the onions, carrots, celery, thyme, parsley, bay leaf, and peppercorns. Bring to a boil, reduce the heat, and simmer for $1\frac{1}{2}$ to 2 hours, skimming fat and foam from the surface as necessary, until reduced to 4 cups.

3 Pour the stock into a fine sieve and strain, extracting as much liquid as possible. Discard the solids. Cool to tepid (this can be done by plunging the stockpot into a sinkful of ice), cover, and refrigerate for 6 hours or until all fat particles have risen to the top. Spoon off solidified fat and discard. Heat the stock over medium-high heat for about 30 minutes. Adjust the seasonings and use as directed in recipe.

4 To store, cool to tepid, cover, and refrigerate for 2 to 3 days or freeze in 1-cup quantities (for ease of use) for up to 3 months.

BEEF, LAMB OR VEAL STOCK

MAKES ABOUT 3 QUARTS
PREPARATION TIME: ABOUT 40 MINUTES
COOKING TIME: ABOUT 7 HOURS

¼ cup plus 2 tablespoons vegetable oil
4 pounds beef, lamb, or veal marrow bones, cut into 2-inch pieces
3 onions, peeled and quartered
1 carrot, peeled and chopped
1 rib celery, chopped
1 tomato, quartered
1 bay leaf
1 tablespoon black peppercorns
2 sprigs fresh thyme
3 cloves garlic, crushed
Approximately 1 gallon (16 cups) water

1 Preheat the oven to 450 degrees F.

2 Using ¼ cup of oil, lightly oil the bones. Spread the bones in a single layer in a large roasting pan. Roast the bones, turning occasionally, for 20 minutes, or until bones are dark golden-brown on all sides.

3 Transfer the bones to a large saucepan or stockpot. Add the remaining oil to roasting pan and stir in the onions, carrot, celery, and tomato. Cook on top of the stove for about 15 minutes over medium-high heat until brown, stirring frequently.

4 With a slotted spoon, transfer the vegetables to the stockpot. Add the bay leaf, peppercorns, thyme, and garlic.

5 Pour off the fat from the roasting pan and discard. Return the pan to moderate heat and deglaze it with 2 cups of water, scraping up any particles sticking to the bottom. Remove from the heat and add this liquid to the stockpot. Pour enough of the remaining water into the stockpot to cover the bones by 2 inches. Bring to a boil, reduce the heat, and let the stock barely simmer, uncovered, for 6 hours, skimming fat and foam from the surface as necessary. Remove from the heat. Cool slightly and chill in the refrigerator for 12 hours or overnight.

6 Pour the stock into a fine sieve into a clean pan. Discard the solids. Spoon off any trace of fat. Place stockpot over high heat and bring stock to a rolling boil. Lower heat and simmer for 30 minutes or until flavor is full-bodied and liquid has slightly reduced. Use as directed in the recipe.

7 To store, cool to tepid (this can be done by plunging the stockpot into a sinkful of ice), cover, and refrigerate for 2 to 3 days or freeze in 1-cup quantities (for ease of use) for up to 3 months.

Fish Stock

MAKES ABOUT 3 CUPS
PREPARATION TIME: ABOUT 20 MINUTES
COOKING TIME: ABOUT 25 MINUTES

Making fish stock is easier and faster than making chicken or beef stock. Substituting a canned broth is tricky in recipes calling for fish stock, but if you have no time to make stock, substitute low-sodium canned chicken broth for fish stock.

2 sprigs fresh parsley
2 sprigs fresh thyme
1 small bay leaf
2 pounds fish bones (saltwater fish such as sole, John Dory, turbot, halibut, or other very fresh, non-oily fish), cut into pieces
2 tablespoons canola or other flavorless oil
1 small onion, chopped
1 small rib celery, chopped
1 cup dry white wine

1 Make a bouquet garni by tying together with kitchen twine the parsley, thyme, and bay leaf. Set aside.

2 Clean the fish bones under cold running water.

3 Heat the oil in a large saucepan or stockpot over medium heat. Add the fish bones and vegetables. Lower the heat and lay a piece of wax paper directly on bones and vegetables in the pan. Cook for 10 minutes, stirring once or twice to prevent browning. Be careful not to push the paper into the pan.

4 Remove the wax paper. Add the wine and enough water to cover the bones and vegetables by 2 inches. Add the bouquet garni. Increase the heat to high and bring to a boil. Skim the surface of all foam. Lower the heat and simmer for 20 to 25 minutes.

5 Strain the stock through an extra-fine sieve. Discard the solids. Use as directed in recipe or cool to tepid (this can be done by plunging the stockpot into a sinkful of ice), cover tightly, and refrigerate for 2 to 3 days or freeze in 1-cup quantities (for ease of use) for up to 3 weeks.

Vegetable Stock

MAKES ABOUT 3 CUPS
PREPARATION TIME: ABOUT 20 MINUTES
COOKING TIME: ABOUT 2 HOURS

Making vegetable stock is easy and fast. Substituting a canned broth is difficult, as finding a good one can be a problem. Low-sodium vegetable bouillon cubes, sold in health food stores, are a good substitute. Low-sodium canned chicken broth can also be used in recipes calling for vegetable stock.

3 quarts cold water
1 carrot, peeled and chopped
1 potato, peeled and chopped
1 large onion, chopped
3 ribs celery, chopped
½ leek, white part only, chopped
1 small tomato, chopped
1 tablespoon salt or to taste
2 cloves garlic, peeled
1 teaspoon chopped fresh parsley
½ teaspoon black peppercorns

1 In a 5-quart saucepan, bring 1 cup of the water to a boil over medium-high heat. Add the carrot, potato, onions, celery, leeks, tomato, and salt. Cook for 5 minutes, stirring occasionally.

2 Add the remaining 11 cups of water to the pan, along with the garlic, parsley, and peppercorns. Bring to a simmer, reduce the heat to low, and simmer gently for 2 hours.

3 Strain the liquid through a fine sieve into a bowl. Discard the vegetables. Let cool for 1 hour and then pour the stock through a fine sieve again. Use as directed in the recipe.

4 To store, cover and refrigerate for up to 3 days or freeze in 1-cup quantities (for ease of use) for up to 3 months.

AUTUMN ELEGANCE—
A DINNER WITH A HINT OF FRANCE

Acorn and Butternut Squash Soup with Roasted Chestnuts
SOUPE DE COURGES AUX MARRONS RÔTIS

Guinea Hen with Quince Purée and Chanterelles
PINTADE À LA PURÉE DE QUOINGS ET AUX CHANTERELLES

Deep Chocolate Marquise
MARQUISE PROFONDE DE CHOCOLAT

WINE SUGGESTIONS:

Light-bodied Champagne (*first course*)

White Burgundy or Viognier (*second course*)

Late Bottled Vintage Port (*dessert*)

WHAT YOU CAN PREPARE AHEAD OF TIME

Up to 1 week ahead: Prepare the Chicken Stock (if making your own).

The day before: Make the quince purée and the mushroom liquid for the Guinea Hen. Cover separately and refrigerate. Make the Chocolate Marquise. Cover and refrigerate.

Early in the day: Make the chestnut purée for the Acorn and Butternut Squash Soup. Fry the celery leaves for the soup garnish (see recipe tip on page 19 in case of damp weather).

David Bouley came to De Gustibus very early in his cooking career to assist Alain Sailhac, then chef at Le Cirque in New York City. Soon after, American-born David left Le Cirque to become head chef of a restaurant in San Francisco opened by Roger Vergé, the esteemed French chef. When Chef Vergé taught one of our classes, David returned to New York to cook with him, and we once again had the pleasure of his talents at the school.

Shortly thereafter, David returned to New York City. Within a couple of years, he had opened Bouley, a restaurant that reflects his love of France and has the feeling of a French country inn. Anyone who follows the New York restaurant scene knows how quickly David garnered four-star accolades for his innovative food. Over the years, Bouley has remained at the top of New York's favorite restaurant list. David Bouley has returned to demonstrate many classes at De Gustibus. His enthusiasm, his knowledge of culinary techniques, and his imaginative way of combining the classic with the revolutionary continue to delight audiences.

◁ Deep Chocolate Marquise (recipe on page 21)

Acorn and Butternut Squash Soup with Roasted Chestnuts

Soupe de Courges aux Marrons Rôtis

This is an aromatic soup combining the rich, sweet taste of our American fall squashes with the intense flavor of the roasted French chestnut, all accented by the innovative use of celery water and crisp celery leaves.

1 pound fresh chestnuts
3 one-pound acorn squash, halved and seeded
3 one-and-one-half-pound butternut squash, halved and seeded
¼ teaspoon freshly grated nutmeg
¼ teaspoon ground cinnamon
1 teaspoon ground mace
2 tablespoons light brown sugar
¼ cup honey
8 tablespoons unsalted butter, melted
2 quarts water
1 rib celery, chopped
Salt and freshly ground white pepper to taste
½ cup celery leaves (optional)
1 cup vegetable oil (if using celery leaves)
¼ cup heavy cream, softly whipped
2 tablespoons minced fresh lemon thyme

■ Special Equipment: chinois; deep-fry thermometer

1 Preheat the oven to 350 degrees F. Assemble the *mise en place* trays for this recipe (see page 9).

2 With a sharp knife cut an "×" on one end of each chestnut and place on a baking sheet. Bake for about 20 minutes, until the chestnuts open and the flesh is tender. Transfer to a plate and allow to cool slightly.

3 When the chestnuts are cool enough to handle, peel with a small sharp knife or your fingers. Put the peeled chestnuts in a small saucepan and cover with water. Bring to a simmer and cook for 5 to 6 minutes, until the flesh is soft. Drain and press the flesh through a chinois or other fine sieve into a medium bowl. Set aside.

4 Meanwhile, place the squash halves, cut side up, in a large shallow baking dish. Dust with the nutmeg, cinnamon, mace, and brown sugar. Drizzle with the honey and

DAVID BOULEY: **Acorn and Butternut Squash Soup with Roasted Chestnuts**

melted butter. Cover the dish tightly with aluminum foil. Bake for 40 minutes, or until tender.

5 In a medium-sized saucepan, combine the chopped celery and the water, and bring to a boil over medium-high heat. Reduce the heat and simmer for 45 minutes. Strain, discarding the solids. Set the celery water aside.

6 Remove the squash from the oven and scrape the flesh from the skin. Process the squash in a food processor just until almost smooth; there will be some lumps. Press the flesh through a chinois or other fine sieve into a medium-sized saucepan. Slowly stir in the reserved celery water. Season to taste with salt and white pepper.

7 Place the soup over medium heat and simmer for about 4 minutes, or until just heated through.

8 Meanwhile, if using, rinse the celery leaves and pat dry with paper towels. In a small saucepan, heat the oil to 325 degrees F. on a deep-fry thermometer. Fry the leaves for 15 seconds, or until crisp. Lift from the oil with a slotted metal spoon or tongs and drain on paper towels.

9 Fold the whipped cream into the reserved chestnut purée. Stir in the lemon thyme.

10 Ladle the soup into 6 warm soup bowls. Using 2 table-spoons, shape the chestnut mixture into 6 small ovals, placing one in the center of each serving. Garnish with the fried celery leaves, if using, and serve.

▶ You may use 8 ounces canned unsweetened chestnut purée, but you will not get the same roasted flavor you will get when you roast the chestnuts yourself.

▶ If you are using the fried celery leaves as a garnish, choose pale, tender leaves. Fry them until crisp, but not brown. Store, uncovered, at room temperature, for up to 6 hours. However, if weather is damp, do not fry any earlier than 1 hour before use, or they will wilt.

▶ A chinois is a fine-meshed cone-shaped French sieve. While other fine-meshed sieves can be used when a chinois is called for, the result may not be as fine in texture. The shape enables the cook to press as much flavor from the solid ingredients as possible because the solids adhere to the sides of the sieve, making it easy to press against them with the back of a spoon.

Guinea Hen with Quince Purée and Chanterelles

SERVES 6
PREPARATION TIME: ABOUT 30 MINUTES
COOKING TIME: ABOUT 2 HOURS

Pintade à la Purée de Quoings et aux Chanterelles

Quinces are fall fruits, related to apples and pears, but they cannot be eaten raw. When cooked, they provide the perfect accent to many dishes. Look for firm, yellow-skinned fruit and store in a cool, dry place—but not the refrigerator. To capture the true essence of Chef Bouley's dish, buy chanterelles from Nova Scotia, if possible.

2 pounds button mushrooms, wiped clean, trimmed, and chopped
2 quarts water
6 large quinces, peeled, quartered, and seeded
6 cups Chicken Stock (see page 13)
1/3 cup chopped celery
1/3 cup chopped carrot
1/3 cup chopped onion
1 sprig fresh thyme
1 bay leaf
1/8 teaspoon dried marjoram

Salt and freshly ground black pepper to taste
3 two-and-one-half-pound guinea hens
1 teaspoon walnut oil
2 pounds chanterelles, wiped clean, trimmed, and sliced
8 shallots, minced
1/4 cup fresh tarragon leaves
1 roasted clove garlic (see page 13)

■ Special Equipment: chinois

1 Assemble the *mise en place* trays for this recipe (see page 9).

2 In a medium-sized saucepan, combine the button mushrooms and water over medium-high heat. Bring to a boil. Reduce the heat and simmer for about 45 minutes, or until the liquid has reduced to 1/2 cup. Strain into a bowl, pressing on the mushrooms. Discard the solids and reserve the liquid.

3 Meanwhile, in a medium-sized saucepan combine the quinces, chicken stock, celery, carrot, onion, thyme, bay leaf, and marjoram. Bring to a boil over medium-high heat. Reduce the heat and simmer for 25 to 30 minutes, until the quinces are very soft. Drain the liquid and reserve for another use. Discard the thyme and bay leaf. Pass the remaining solids through a chinois or other fine sieve into a small saucepan. Taste and adjust the seasoning with salt and pepper. Set aside.

4 Preheat the oven to 375 degrees F.

5 Generously season the guinea hens with salt and pepper. Put in a shallow pan and roast for about 45 minutes, or until cooked through and the juices run clear when the flesh is pricked with the tip of a sharp knife. Remove from the oven and let rest for 10 minutes before carving.

6 While the hens are roasting, heat the walnut oil in a large sauté pan over medium heat. Add the chanterelles, shallots, and tarragon. Sauté for about 10 minutes, or until the vegetables are very soft. Push the roasted garlic pulp from the skin and add to the chanterelles. Add the reserved mushroom liquid and stir to combine. Remove from the heat and keep warm.

7 Place the quince purée over low heat just to warm through.

8 Using a boning knife, remove the breast halves from the hens. Slice each half, diagonally, into thin slices. Remove the legs with the thighs attached.

9 Spoon the warm quince purée into the centers of 6 warm dinner plates. Arrange a sliced breast half around one side of each serving of purée. Lay the legs on the other side. Arrange the chanterelle mixture on top of the breast meat, and drizzle some of the liquid from the chanterelles over all. Serve immediately.

DAVID BOULEY: Guinea Hen with Quince Purée and Chanterelles

▶ When buying walnut oil, purchase the smallest quantity possible, as it is expensive and it turns rancid very rapidly. A small amount of this flavorful oil adds a distinctive, nutty fragrance to vinaigrettes, baked goods containing walnuts, sautés, or sauces. Store tightly covered in the refrigerator. It usually does not keep for longer than 2 months.

▶ You can substitute small chickens, pheasants, or Rock Cornish game hens for guinea hens.

Deep Chocolate Marquise

Marquise Profonde de Chocolat

This rich, dark, luxurious chocolate dessert is a true indulgence. Use the best bittersweet chocolate you can find for the most intense flavor.

LADYFINGERS:

8 large eggs, separated
1½ cups plus 2 tablespoons granulated sugar
⅞ cup all-purpose flour
⅞ cup cornstarch
2 teaspoons pure coffee extract
2 teaspoons pure vanilla extract

MARQUISE:

6 large egg yolks
1¼ cups plus 2 tablespoons confectioners' sugar
8 ounces bittersweet chocolate, coarsely chopped
1 cup unsalted butter
2 tablespoons orange-flavored liqueur, such as Cointreau or Grand Marnier
Grated zest of 2 oranges (about 2 tablespoons)
½ cup Dutch-processed cocoa powder
1¼ cups heavy cream, softly whipped
Whipped cream, for garnish
6 fresh mint sprigs, for garnish

1 Assemble the *mise en place* trays for this recipe (see page 9). Preheat the oven to 325 degrees F. Lightly butter and flour 2 baking sheets. Lightly butter an 8-inch spring-form pan.

2 To make the ladyfingers, using an electric mixer set on medium-high speed, beat the egg yolks with 1 cup plus 2 tablespoons of sugar for 3 to 4 minutes until pale yellow and thick.

3 In another bowl, using an electric mixer set on medium-high speed, beat the egg whites and the remaining ½ cup of sugar until stiff and shiny.

4 Whisk together the flour and cornstarch. Fold the dry ingredients into the egg yolk mixture, alternating with the meringue. When well combined, divide the mixture in half. Stir coffee extract into one half of the batter and vanilla extract into the other half.

5 Spoon the coffee-flavored batter into a pastry bag fitted with a plain tip. Pipe batter onto the baking sheets, making 4-inch strips about ½ inch apart. When all the coffee batter is gone, fill the pastry bag with the vanilla batter and make more ladyfingers.

6 Bake for about 15 minutes until light golden. Cool the ladyfingers completely on wire racks.

7 To make the marquise, put the egg yolks and confectioners' sugar in a medium-sized bowl set over a larger bowl filled with very warm water. Using a hand-held electric mixer set on medium speed, beat until well mixed. Increase the speed to medium-high and beat for 4 to 5 minutes until the mixture is pale yellow and thick. Remove from the water and set aside.

8 In the top half of a double boiler, melt the chocolate over barely simmering water. Transfer to a large bowl and set aside.

9 In a small saucepan, melt the butter over medium-low heat. Stir in the liqueur and orange zest.

10 Whisk the butter mixture into the chocolate, alternating with the cocoa. When well blended, fold in the beaten egg yolk mixture. Fold in the whipped cream.

11 Line the sides of the springform pan with alternating flavors of ladyfingers, positioning them so that they stand up straight around the pan. Spoon the chocolate marquise mixture into the pan and smooth the top with a spatula. Cover with plastic wrap and refrigerate for at least 4 hours.

12 To serve, carefully remove the sides of the springform pan. Slice the cake and serve each piece with whipped cream and a sprig of mint.

▶ **You can substitute high-quality ladyfingers sold in French bakeries for homemade ladyfingers. They also are sold packaged in specialty stores. Be sure to buy slender, French-style ladyfingers rather than plump, American style.**

A Lovely Lunch or Sunday Supper

Curried Cream of Cauliflower and Apple Soup
SOUPE CRÈME DE CHOUX-FLEURS ET POMME AU CURRY

Beef Shank Terrine with Leeks and Horseradish Sauce
TERRINE DE BOEUF AUX POIREAUX AVEC SAUCE AU RAIFORT

Warm Apricot Tarts with Pistachios
TARTE TATIN AUX ABRICOTS ET À LA PISTACHE

WINE SUGGESTIONS:

Alsace or California Sparkling Wine (*first course*)

Red Burgundy or Pomerol (*second course*)

Muscat de Beaumes-de-Venise or German Auslese Riesling (*dessert*)

WHAT YOU CAN PREPARE AHEAD OF TIME

Up to 1 week ahead: Prepare the Chicken Stock (if making your own).

Up to 3 days ahead: Prepare the Beef Terrine. Wrap in plastic and refrigerate.

Up to 1 day ahead: Make the Curried Cream of Cauliflower and Apple Soup. Cool, then cover and refrigerate. Reheat over medium heat.

Early in the day: Prepare the apple garnish for the soup. Reheat in the top of a double boiler. Make the Horseradish Sauce. Make the Apricot Tarts. Do not cover them with pastry or unmold them until just before serving.

I first met Daniel Boulud when he was a sous-chef at the Polo restaurant in New York. Although very young at the time, he was already an accomplished chef, having begun his training as a fourteen-year-old apprentice in France.

Daniel taught his first demonstration class when he became the executive chef at La Régence, the French-style restaurant at New York's Hotel Plaza Athenée. We were all awed by his abilities. Now owner of his own restaurant, Daniel, on the East Side of Manhattan, Chef Boulud always puts a great deal of thought into the kitchen skills and tricks he shares with home cooks. Consequently, we are consistently thrilled by his classes. His support of the efforts of De Gustibus has been a boon to our students in understanding what great French cooking is all about.

◁ Beef Shank Terrine with Leeks and Horseradish Sauce (recipe on page 25)

Curried Cream of Cauliflower and Apple Soup

Soupe Crème de Choux-Fleurs et Pomme au Curry

Smooth and creamy with a sweet, spicy taste, this soup is the perfect starter to any festive meal. The fact that it can be prepared a day in advance and reheated at the last minute makes it an even better first course for the busy host or hostess. The soup is also tasty served cold.

4 cups Chicken Stock (see page 13)
1½ tablespoons unsalted butter
1 cup chopped onions
2 teaspoons curry powder
¾ teaspoon saffron threads (or saffron powder)
1 cup sliced tart apples, such as Granny Smith
4 cups cauliflower florets
1 cup heavy cream
Salt and freshly ground white pepper to taste

GARNISH:

1 cup diced tart apples, such as Granny Smith
1 tablespoon water
1 teaspoon curry powder
¼ teaspoon saffron threads (or saffron powder)
Salt and freshly ground white pepper to taste
1 tablespoon chopped fresh chives

1 Assemble the *mise en place* trays for this recipe (see page 9).

2 In a medium-sized saucepan, warm the stock over low heat.

3 In a large saucepan, melt the butter over medium heat. Add the onions, curry powder, and saffron and cook, stirring frequently, for about 2 minutes, until the onions begin to soften. Add the sliced apples and cook, stirring frequently, for 5 minutes. Stir in the cauliflower and warm chicken stock, increase the heat, and bring to a boil. Reduce the heat and simmer for 20 to 30 minutes, until the cauliflower is very tender.

4 Transfer the soup, in batches if necessary, to a blender or a food processor fitted with the metal blade and process until very smooth. Pour into a medium-sized saucepan and stir in the cream. Season to taste with salt and white pepper and keep warm over very low heat.

5 To make the garnish, combine the diced apples and water in a small saucepan over medium heat and bring to a simmer. Stir in the curry powder and saffron, and season to taste with salt and white pepper. Cover and cook for about 3 minutes. Strain through a fine sieve, reserving the solids. Return the apples to the pan to keep warm.

6 Ladle the soup into warm soup bowls. Sprinkle the diced apple and chopped chives over the top.

DANIEL BOULUD: Curried Cream of Cauliflower and Apple Soup

Beef Shank Terrine with Leeks and Horseradish Sauce

SERVES 6
PREPARATION TIME: ABOUT 45 MINUTES
COOKING TIME: ABOUT 2 HOURS AND 30 MINUTES
CHILLING TIME: 24 HOURS

Terrine de Boeuf aux Poireaux avec Sauce au Raifort

This terrine is great on its own as a light summer lunch, served with a salad, a crisp baguette, a bowl of fresh fruit—and, of course, a light French wine!

10 pounds well trimmed beef shank, cut into large pieces, or 1 whole beef shank, well trimmed
2 carrots, peeled and chopped
2 ribs celery, chopped
1 sprig fresh thyme
2 whole cloves
1 bay leaf
1 tablespoon salt, or to taste
5 peppercorns
10 large leeks, washed, trimmed, and green part removed
1½ tablespoons unflavored gelatin
2 tablespoons cold water
2 tablespoons fresh tarragon leaves
Freshly ground black pepper
Horseradish Sauce (recipe follows)
½ cup peeled, seeded, and diced tomatoes
1 tablespoon minced fresh chives

■ Special Equipment: 12 x 4 x 4-inch terrine mold or loaf pan

1 Assemble the *mise en place* trays for this recipe (see page 9).

2 Put the beef in a large heavy saucepan and add enough cold water to cover. Bring to a boil, reduce the heat to low, and simmer for 30 minutes, skimming the surface frequently.

3 Add the carrots, celery, thyme, cloves, bay leaf, salt, and peppercorns, and simmer for 1½ hours.

4 Meanwhile, tie a piece of kitchen twine around each leek to hold it together. Distribute the leeks around the beef. Cover and cook for 30 to 45 minutes longer, or until meat is fork-tender. Remove from the heat and let the meat cool slightly in the liquid.

5 Using a slotted spoon, carefully remove the leeks from the pan. Untie them, place in a shallow dish, and set aside.

DANIEL BOULUD: Beef Shank Terrine with Leeks and Horseradish Sauce

6 Carefully transfer the beef shank to a shallow dish, and set aside.

7 Strain the stock through a coarse sieve, and discard the solids. Strain again through an extra-fine sieve. Skim the fat from the surface of the stock. (Or refrigerate it for several hours and then lift the hardened fat from the surface.)

8 Measure 2 cups of the stock into a small saucepan and heat over very low heat. Reserve the remaining stock for another purpose.

DANIEL BOULUD: Individual serving of Beef Shank Terrine with Leeks and Horseradish Sauce

9 Meanwhile, in a small bowl, combine the gelatin and cold water and let sit for about 5 minutes, or until softened. Stir the gelatin into the hot stock until dissolved. Add the tarragon and season to taste with salt and pepper. Set aside and keep warm.

10 Line a 12 x 4 x 4-inch terrine mold with plastic wrap, allowing about a 3-inch overhang all around.

11 Pull the meat from the bones, breaking it into small pieces. Put a layer of meat on the bottom of the terrine. Arrange whole leeks in 2 parrallel lines down the pan. Continue making alternate layers of meat and leeks, finishing with a layer of meat.

12 Pour the hot stock mixture over the terrine, pressing down with a spatula to make sure it is evenly distributed in the mold. Fold the plastic wrap up over the top to cover. Refrigerate for 24 hours.

13 To unmold, open the plastic wrap and use it to lift the terrine out of the mold. Unwrap the terrine and discard the plastic wrap. Cut the terrine into ¾-inch-thick slices using an electric knife or a very sharp serrated knife.

14 Place 2 slices of the terrine on each serving plate. Spoon a little Horseradish Sauce around the edge, and garnish with the diced tomatoes and chives.

▶ **To produce a really clear jellied stock, line the sieve with a double thickness of cheesecloth before straining the stock the second time.**

HORSERADISH SAUCE
Sauce au Raifort

This sauce also makes a good condiment for grilled or broiled fish or chicken.

MAKES ABOUT 3 CUPS
PREPARATION TIME: ABOUT 20 MINUTES, PLUS CHILLING

2½ cups heavy cream
2 tablespoons Dijon mustard
1 teaspoon dry mustard
¼ cup sherry wine vinegar
3 tablespoons freshly grated horseradish
1 tablespoon chopped cornichons
1 tablespoon chopped capers
1 tablespoon chopped fresh parsley
1 tablespoon chopped fresh chives
Salt and freshly ground black pepper to taste

1 In a medium-sized bowl, beat the cream, mustards, and vinegar together until well combined.

2 Stir in the horseradish, cornichons, capers, parsley, and chives. Season to taste with salt and pepper. Cover and refrigerate until ready to use.

▶ **Freshly grated horseradish can be replaced with very well-drained bottled white horseradish.**

Warm Apricot Tarts with Pistachios

Tarte Tatin aux Abricots et à la Pistache

These tarts taste great made with canned apricots, but you could, in the height of summer, use fresh ones. Or, substitute fresh peaches or nectarines. If you want to make these tarts ahead of time, unmold them while they are still warm—otherwise, the caramel sets and they are impossible to remove from the molds.

1½ pounds frozen puff pastry, thawed
¾ cup plus 1 tablespoon granulated sugar
¼ cup water
¼ cup heavy cream
9 canned whole apricots or 18 apricot halves packed in water, drained, halved, and pitted (if whole)
1 pint high-quality vanilla ice cream
1 tablespoon chopped, toasted pistachios
6 fresh mint sprigs, for garnish

■ Special Equipment: 6 three-inch round tart molds; 3-inch plain cutter

1 Preheat the oven to 375 degrees F. Lightly butter 6 three-inch round tart molds and set the molds on a baking sheet. Assemble the *mise en place* trays for this recipe (see page 9).

2 On a lightly floured surface, roll out the pastry almost paper-thin. Transfer to a baking sheet and prick all over with a fork. Bake for 20 minutes, or until golden. Remove from the oven, and reduce the oven temperature to 350 degrees F.

3 In a heavy saucepan, combine the sugar and water and bring to a boil over medium heat, stirring occasionally until the sugar is dissolved. Lower the heat to a simmer and let the syrup cook for 30 to 40 minutes, without stirring, until it is a deep golden brown. Swirl the syrup occasionally by tilting the pan, but take care, as sugar syrup is very hot.

4 Remove the pan from the heat and carefully stir in the heavy cream. The hot syrup may spatter. Stir until smooth and then pour into the tart molds.

5 Place 3 apricot halves, rounded side up, in an overlapping pattern in each mold. Bake for 5 minutes.

6 Meanwhile, using a 3-inch plain cutter, cut 6 circles from the puff pastry.

7 Remove the molds from the oven and lay a pastry circle on top of each one. Immediately invert the tarts onto warm dessert plates.

8 Place a small scoop of vanilla ice cream in the center of each tart. Sprinkle each one with pistachios, garnish with a mint leaf, and serve.

▶ High-quality vanilla ice cream tastes richer and creamier because it is. According to federal guidelines, ice cream manufacturers can incorporate a certain amount of air into their product: the better the quality, the less air—and the higher the cost. Less air means more cream, flavorings, and, in most cases, care.

DANIEL BOULUD: Warm Apricot Tarts with Pistachios

A Tribute to the End of Summer

Tomato Tart with Lime Butter
TARTE AUX TOMATES ET BEURRE DE CITRONS VERTS

Red Snapper with Tomatoes and Caramelized Garlic
ROUGET À LA TOMATE ET AIL CARAMELISÉ

Chicken in Parchment with Thyme
POULET EN PAPILLOTE AU THYM

Sweet Green Tomato Pie
TARTE DOUCE DE TOMATES VERTES

WINE SUGGESTION:

Sauvignon Blanc

WHAT YOU CAN PREPARE AHEAD OF TIME

Up to 1 week ahead: Prepare the Chicken Stock (if making your own).

Early in the day: Prepare the filling for the Tomato Tart. Cover and refrigerate. Bake the pastry shell and make the filling for the Sweet Tomato Pie. Prepare garlic, tomatoes, and onions for the Red Snapper. Cover separately and refrigerate. Assemble the chicken and thyme packets. Refrigerate.

In the afternoon: Line the tart pan for the Tomato Tart. Refrigerate.

Just before serving: Make the Lime Butter for the Tomato Tart. Keep warm in a double boiler.

I was first introduced to Antoine Bouterin by the late Gregory Usher, then of the famous French cooking school La Varenne. Antoine had just moved to New York and Gregory felt that we at De Gustibus should experience this great French chef's talents and food. Great he was in the kitchen—but he was not so great with the English language. However, with a translator at his side, Antoine performed miracles and the class was, as Gregory had promised, a rousing success. As Chef Bouterin's reputation grew in America, so did his command of English, and he has returned to teach many times, without a translator. We like nothing better than to lure him from his kitchen at Le Périgord, a New York City restaurant, to share his food and skills with our students. The food is redolent with the flavors of his native Provence, and equally warming is his sunny Provençal disposition. This menu is especially interesting in that the chef showcases tomatoes, at their very best at the end of the summer, in every recipe.

◁ Chicken in Parchment with Thyme (recipe on page 33)

Tomato Tart with Lime Butter

SERVES 6
PREPARATION TIME: ABOUT 35 MINUTES
BAKING TIME: ABOUT 30 MINUTES

Tarte aux Tomates et Beurre de Citrons Verts

This tart is not only a sensational first course, but would also be a wonderful brunch or light lunch entrée.

TART:

½ pound frozen puff pastry, thawed
2 pounds ripe tomatoes, cored, peeled, seeded, and finely chopped
Juice of 1 large lemon
2 shallots, minced
2 cloves garlic, minced
½ teaspoon minced fresh parsley
¼ teaspoon minced fresh basil
¼ teaspoon minced fresh thyme
Salt and freshly ground black pepper to taste
2 tablespoons olive oil

LIME BUTTER:

Juice of 1 large lime
8 tablespoons unsalted butter, cut into tablespoon-size pieces
2 tablespoons heavy cream
Salt and freshly ground black pepper to taste
½ cup peeled, seeded, and diced ripe tomatoes, for garnish

■ Special Equipment: six 4-inch tartlet pans (not with removable bottoms); pastry weights, dried beans, or rice

1 Preheat the oven to 400 degrees F. Assemble the *mise en place* trays for this recipe (see page 9).

2 On a floured surface, roll out the pastry to approximately a 15-inch square. Using a sharp knife, cut the pastry into six 5¼-inch squares. Gently fit each square into a 4-inch tartlet pan. Trim the excess dough from the edges. Prick

ANTOINE BOUTERIN:
Tomato Tart with
Lime Butter

30

the bottom of the pastry shelves all over with a fork. Line the pastry shells with aluminum foil cut about 2 inches larger than the pan so that there is no overhang. Spread pastry weights, dried beans, or rice over the foil. Set the tartlet pan on a baking sheet and bake for about 15 minutes, until the pastry is lightly browned. Lift out the foil and weights. Gently lift the baked shells from the tartlet pans and set the pastry shells on a wire rack to cool. Do not turn off the oven.

3 Meanwhile, put the tomatoes in a colander and let drain for about 15 minutes. Pat dry with paper towels.

4 In a glass or ceramic bowl, combine the tomatoes, lemon juice, shallots, garlic, parsley, basil, thyme, and salt and pepper to taste. Stir in the olive oil.

5 Put the baking sheet back in the oven for about 5 minutes. Lift the hot sheet from the oven and position the tartlet shells on it. Spoon approximately 2 tablespoons of the tomato mixture into each shell. Do not overfill. Bake for about 15 minutes, or until centers are firm. As the tartlets

bake, pat the filling with paper towel 2 or 3 times to absorb excess liquid. Grind a light coating of pepper over the top of each tartlet. Let cool for 5 minutes before serving.

6 Meanwhile, make the lime butter: In a small nonreactive saucepan, combine the lime juice with an equal amount of water (about ⅓ cup). Bring to a boil over high heat, and boil for about 3 minutes, or until reduced by half. Whisk in the butter, a tablespoon at a time, until well incorporated. Stir in the cream and season to taste with salt and pepper. Pour into the top half of a double boiler and place over hot water to keep warm.

7 Spoon the lime butter onto plates. Set the tartlets on top, and garnish with the diced tomatoes. Serve immediately.

▶It's important to let the tomatoes drain to remove excess moisture and then to blot them during baking. Have the paper towels ready—folded two or three thick—before opening the oven door. Work quickly so as not to let too much heat escape.

Red Snapper with Tomatoes and Caramelized Garlic

Rouget à la Tomate et Ail Caramelisé

SERVES 6
PREPARATION TIME: ABOUT 15 MINUTES
COOKING TIME: ABOUT 1 HOUR

This dish epitomizes the sunny flavors of Provence. Without doubt, it is a dish for garlic-lovers.

3 pounds red snapper fillets, skinned
6 tablespoons peanut oil
22 cloves garlic, peeled (2 to 3 heads)
2 tablespoons sugar
6 large ripe tomatoes, cored, peeled, seeded, and chopped
1 large onion, thinly sliced
1 cup Chicken Stock (see page 13)
½ teaspoon minced fresh thyme
3 large, fresh basil leaves, minced
2 large, fresh sage leaves, minced
1 bay leaf
Pinch of ground cumin
Salt and freshly ground black pepper to taste
6 sprigs fresh parsley

1 Assemble the *mise en place* trays for this recipe (see page 9).

2 Remove any bones from the fish, rinse it, and pat dry with paper towels. Cut into 2-inch chunks. Cover and refrigerate until ready to cook.

3 In a small sauté pan, heat 2 tablespoons of the oil over medium heat. Add the garlic cloves and sauté for 6 to 7 minutes, until lightly browned. Stir in the sugar. Cook, stirring continuously, for about 3 minutes, until the garlic is caramelized.

4 Using a slotted spoon, transfer the garlic cloves to a paper towel to drain. Mash 4 of the cloves and set aside. Keep the remaining 18 cloves warm.

5 In a large sauté pan, heat 2 tablespoons of the oil over medium heat. Add the chopped tomatoes and cook, stir-

ring frequently, for 20 to 30 minutes, until all the liquid has evaporated. The tomatoes will be smooth and thick. Remove from the heat.

6 In a medium-sized sauté pan, heat the remaining 2 tablespoons of oil over medium heat. Add the onion and sauté for about 5 minutes, until softened and lightly browned. Stir in the mashed garlic, the tomatoes, stock, thyme, basil, sage, bay leaf, cumin, and salt and pepper to taste. Add the fish and cook, stirring occasionally, for about 10 minutes, until cooked through. Remove the bay leaf.

7 Place equal portions of the fish and vegetable sauce in the center of 6 warm dinner plates. Garnish each plate with 3 garlic cloves and a sprig of parsley.

Chicken in Parchment with Thyme

SERVES 6
PREPARATION TIME: ABOUT 15 MINUTES
COOKING TIME: ABOUT 25 MINUTES

Poulet en Papillote au Thym

This recipe calls for cooking the chicken in parchment, but heavy-duty aluminum foil is an easy and accessible option for the home cook. The foil packets can also be placed on the grill for perfect summertime entertaining.

6 skinless, boneless chicken breast halves, trimmed
1 cup chopped leeks, white parts only
½ cup diced celery
1 cup cored, peeled, seeded, and diced tomatoes
Grated zest of 1 lemon
3 cloves garlic, sliced
3 tablespoons chopped scallions
1 tablespoon minced fresh thyme
Salt and freshly ground black pepper to taste
24 to 30 fresh spinach leaves, washed, dried, stems removed
6 tablespoons dry white wine

1 Preheat oven to 400 degrees F. Assemble the *mise en place* trays for this recipe (see page 9).

2 Cut 6 pieces of heavy-duty aluminum foil into rectangles approximately 18 x 20 inches.

3 Rinse the chicken and pat dry with paper towels. Using a cleaver or heavy knife, slightly flatten each breast half.

4 Combine the leeks and celery. Put about ¼ cup of the vegetables toward the bottom edge of each piece of foil. Lay a chicken breast on top, and put 4 to 5 spinach leaves on top of the chicken.

5 Combine the tomatoes, lemon zest, garlic, scallions, thyme, and salt and pepper to taste. Divide this mixture evenly among the packets, spooning it on top of the chicken. Sprinkle 1 tablespoon of the wine over each one.

6 Fold the top half of each sheet of foil over the chicken so that the edges meet like a book. Fold the bottom edges up to make a 1-inch fold. Fold the 1-inch closure in half, making a ½-inch fold, and fold over once more with a ½-inch fold. Fold the sides in the same way. You should have formed a packet, closed tightly around the ingredients. Place on a large baking sheet and bake for 20 to 25 minutes, or until the foil packages swell up. Serve in the packets, letting your guests slit open the foil at the table, and enjoy the fragrant aroma that steams out.

ANTOINE BOUTERIN: **Chicken in Parchment with Thyme**

◁ ANTOINE BOUTERIN: **Red Snapper with Tomatoes and Caramelized Garlic**

Sweet Green Tomato Pie

SERVES 6
PREPARATION TIME: ABOUT 20 MINUTES
BAKING TIME: ABOUT 20 MINUTES

Tarte Douce de Tomates Vertes

This unusual French dessert calls for unripe tomatoes. In rural America, green tomato pie is often served as dessert. In both countries, the recipes were created to utilize bumper crops that gardeners feared would not reach ripeness before the autumn frost. This pie has a wonderful fresh taste, as citrus again heightens the flavor of the tomatoes.

2 lemons
5 tablespoons water
½ cup granulated sugar
½ pound puff pastry, thawed
1 large egg
1 tablespoon arrowroot
4½ tablespoons unsalted butter
3 pounds green tomatoes, cored, peeled, seeded, and sliced into ¼-inch slices
3 large egg whites
1 tablespoon confectioners' sugar

■ Special Equipment: 9-inch tart pan with removable bottom; pastry weights, beans, or rice

1 Preheat the oven to 400 degrees F. Assemble the *mise en place* trays for this recipe (see page 9).

2 Using a sharp knife, carefully remove the yellow-colored peel from 1 of the lemons, avoiding the bitter white pith. Cut the peel into a fine julienne. Grate the zest from the remaining lemon and set aside.

3 In a small saucepan, combine the julienned peel, the water, and 3 tablespoons of the sugar. Bring to a boil over high heat, and cook for 4 to 5 minutes, until all the water has evaporated. Drain the lemon peel on paper towels and set aside.

4 On a lightly floured surface, roll out the pastry to a circle about ⅛ inch thick and approximately 12 inches round. Transfer the pastry to a 9-inch tart pan with a removable bottom. Gently fit the pastry into the pan, and trim off any excess. Prick the bottom of the pastry all over with a fork. Line the pastry shell with aluminum foil and spread pastry weights, dried beans, or rice over the foil. Bake for about 15 minutes, until the pastry is lightly browned. Lift out the foil and weights, and set on a wire rack to cool. Do not turn off the oven.

5 In a small bowl, beat the egg with the arrowroot.

6 In a large sauté pan, melt the butter over medium heat. Cook the tomato slices for about 5 minutes, or until softened, stirring gently every so often and taking care not to tear the slices. Sprinkle 3 tablespoons of the sugar over them and stir gently. Spoon some liquid from the pan into the egg mixture and stir to temper it. Add the egg mixture to the pan, and stir gently. Remove from the heat, and stir in the julienned lemon peel. Pour this mixture into the partially baked pastry shell, and let the filling cool slightly.

7 In a large bowl, using an electric mixer, beat the egg whites until soft peaks form. Add the remaining 2 tablespoons of sugar and beat until stiff peaks form. Fold the lemon zest into the meringue. Using a spatula, spread the meringue evenly over the tomato filling, swirling and lifting the meringue to make an attractive design.

8 Bake for about 5 minutes, until the meringue is golden. Sprinkle with the confectioners' sugar and serve immediately.

▶ When making a tart with a filling as moist as this one, do not expect the pastry to stay firm and crisp. It will soften a little beneath the filling.

▷ ANTOINE BOUTERIN: Sweet Green Tomato Pie

34

CLASSIC FRENCH FOR FRIENDS

Artichoke Bottoms Filled with Poached Oysters
COEURS D'ARTICHAUTS FARCIES AUX HUÎTRES POCHÉES

Apple Soufflé on a Platter with Apricot Sauce
SOUFFLÉ DE POMMES À L'ASSIETTE AVEC SAUCE AUX ABRICOTS

WINE SUGGESTIONS:

Premier Cru Chablis or California Chardonnay (*first course*)

Late Harvest Muscat or Riesling (*dessert*)

WHAT YOU CAN PREPARE AHEAD OF TIME

Up to 3 days ahead: Prepare and cook the artichokes for the Artichoke Bottoms. Cover and refrigerate.

Up to 2 days ahead: Prepare and cook the diced apples for the Apple Soufflé. Cover and refrigerate. Prepare the Apricot Sauce for the Apple Soufflé. Cover and refrigerate.

The day before: Prepare the croutons for the Apple Soufflé. Cover and refrigerate.

Early in the day: Make the artichoke sauce, leaving out the oysters. Top with a film of heavy cream to prevent drying out. Cover and refrigerate. Prepare the oysters and refrigerate separately. Gently fold into the sauce as it reheats.

Julia Child was one of the very first superstars we invited to teach at De Gustibus. This was during the time when we were still housed in an off-off Broadway theater and our kitchen was composed of two electric burners. Julia arrived with one of her favorite kitchen tools, a blowtorch. During her demonstration, she flamboyantly showed the class how to peel the skins from tomatoes and caramelize a tart using her handy flamethrower!

From the beginning, Julia has been very supportive of our efforts to bring demonstrations by notable chefs to "regular people." She had not visited us for some years until recently, when she came as an honored guest at a special program at De Gustibus. In her own words, "What fun it is to be back at De Gustibus. It has been a number of years and how nice it is to see the advances from that funny little attic theater to this very chic Macy's environment."

Julia Child is truly a remarkable person. This is a very simple menu—only two dishes!—but the flavors are perfectly balanced and the food sublime.

◁ Artichoke Bottoms Filled with Poached Oysters (recipe on page 38)

Artichoke Bottoms Filled with Poached Oysters

Coeurs d'Artichauts Farcies aux Huîtres Pochées

This most traditional French dish is so typically Julia you will love it just as you do all her food. Cream, butter, succulent oysters, and tender artichokes are put together beautifully and served with her trademark, a merry "Bon Appétit!"

¼ cup all-purpose flour
6 cups cold water
¼ cup fresh lemon juice
½ teaspoon salt, or to taste
6 large artichokes with 3-inch bases
1 lemon, halved
2 tablespoons unsalted butter, melted
Freshly ground black pepper to taste
4 tablespoons unsalted butter
1 tablespoon minced shallots
1 pint large fresh shucked oysters in their liquor
½ cup dry white wine or vermouth
1 large egg yolk
½ cup heavy cream
2 tablespoons minced fresh parsley

1 Assemble the *mise en place* trays for this recipe (see page 9).

2 In a medium-sized saucepan, whisk the flour into 3 cups of the water. Stir in the remaining 3 cups of water, the lemon juice, and salt. Bring to a boil over medium-high heat. Remove from the heat and set aside. (This mixture, known as a blanc, will be used to cook the artichokes to insure that they will not discolor.)

3 Cut off the stems of one of the artichokes. Bend the outer leaves back and snap them off, leaving the edible leaf bottoms attached to the base. Continue to remove the leaves, leaving the edible bottoms, until you reach the soft crown of leaves in the center. Cut off this crown of leaves. Using a small sharp knife, trim the base evenly to remove all the greenish parts and create a perfect round. To keep the artichoke from discoloring, frequently rub the cut surfaces with the lemon halves as you work. Drop the arti-

choke into the blanc, and repeat with the remaining artichokes. If the liquid does not cover the artichokes, add additional water as necessary.

4 When all the artichokes are trimmed, place the pan over medium-high heat and bring to a boil. Reduce the heat and simmer for 30 minutes, or until the artichoke bottoms are tender when pierced with a knife.

5 Meanwhile, preheat the oven to 300 degrees F.

6 Drain the artichokes well, and reserve ½ cup of the cooking liquid. Rinse the artichokes under cold running water and dry with paper towels. Scoop out the chokes (fuzzy interior) with a teaspoon and discard. Brush the artichokes with the melted butter and sprinkle with salt and pepper. Place in a shallow baking pan, cover with aluminum foil, and bake for 15 minutes.

7 Meanwhile, in a medium-sized sauté pan, melt the butter over medium heat. Add the shallots and sauté for about 3 minutes, or until just soft. Drain the oysters, reserving the liquor, and cut in half any that are especially large. Add to the pan and cook for 1 minute, or until plumped. Using a slotted spoon, transfer the oysters to a bowl.

8 Add the reserved oyster liquor to the pan. Stir in the wine and the ½ cup of reserved artichoke cooking liquid. Bring to a boil, and cook, stirring frequently, for about 2 minutes, until just thickened.

9 In a medium-sized bowl, whisk the egg yolk and cream together. Add a little of the thickened sauce, whisking continuously. Continue to add the sauce, whisking, until it is all incorporated. Return the sauce to the pan and bring to a simmer over medium heat. Season to taste with salt and pepper.

10 Carefully fold the oysters into the sauce, and remove from the heat.

11 Arrange the artichoke bottoms on a serving platter. Spoon the oysters and sauce into the cavities of the artichokes. Sprinkle with the parsley and serve immediately.

Apple Soufflé on a Platter with Apricot Sauce

SERVES 6
PREPARATION TIME: ABOUT 30 MINUTES
COOKING TIME: ABOUT 30 MINUTES

Soufflé de Pommes à l'Assiette avec Sauce aux Abricots

For this recipe, you need an attractive, ovenproof platter on which you will bake the soufflé and then carry it to the table. This means you need not dig out your soufflé dish! Many of the components can be prepared well in advance, but the soufflé must be baked at the last minute.

12 slices home-style white bread
3 tablespoons clarified butter (see page 12)
7 tablespoons unsalted butter
3 sweet, firm apples, such as Golden Delicious or McIntosh, peeled, cored, and cut into 3/8-inch dice
11 tablespoons granulated sugar
1/4 teaspoon fresh lemon juice
1/4 teaspoon ground cinnamon
1/4 cup Calvados or bourbon
1/4 cup chopped walnuts (optional)
Apricot Sauce (recipe follows)
1 cup milk
1/4 cup cornstarch, sifted
1 tablespoon pure vanilla extract
4 large eggs
5 large egg whites
3 tablespoons confectioners' sugar

■ Special Equipment: 8 x 11-inch ovenproof platter; 3-inch round cutter

1 Assemble the *mise en place* trays for this recipe (see page 9).

2 To make the croûtons for the soufflé, use a 3-inch round cutter to cut a round out of each slice of bread.

3 In a medium-sized, nonstick sauté pan, heat the clarified butter over medium heat. Add the bread rounds and sauté, turning once, for 3 to 4 minutes, until golden on both sides. Drain the croûtons on paper towels.

4 In a medium-sized, nonstick saucepan, heat 3 tablespoons of the butter over medium heat. Add the apples and sauté for about 5 minutes, or until almost soft. Stir in 4 tablespoons of the sugar, the lemon juice, and cinnamon. Sauté for about 5 minutes longer, until the apples begin to

caramelize. Add the Calvados, increase the heat, and boil rapidly for about 3 minutes, swirling the apples around in the pan, until all the liquid has evaporated. Remove from the heat and stir in the walnuts, if desired. Set aside.

5 Place a rack in the upper third of the oven, and preheat the oven to 425 degrees F. Using 1 tablespoon of butter, butter an 8 x 11-inch ovenproof platter.

6 Spread a little of the Apricot Sauce over each croûton. Arrange them on the buttered platter. Spoon the apples on the croûtons, and top each with a dollop of sauce.

7 In a medium-sized saucepan, whisk the milk into the cornstarch until smooth. Set over medium heat, and whisk in 5 tablespoons of the remaining sugar and the remaining 3 tablespoons of butter. Cook, stirring continuously, for about 4 minutes, or until the mixture comes to a boil. If lumps form, boil for 1 minute longer, beating vigorously until smooth. Remove from the heat and stir in the vanilla. The mixture will be thick and gluey. Beat in the egg yolks, one at a time.

8 In a large bowl, using an electric mixer, beat the egg whites with the remaining 2 tablespoons of sugar until stiff, shiny peaks form. Stir about a quarter of the egg whites into egg yolk mixture to loosen it. Then, carefully and rapidly, fold in the remaining egg whites.

9 Mound the soufflé mixture over the fruit-topped croûtons. Bake for about 12 minutes, or until the soufflé has risen and started to brown. Quickly sprinkle the top of the soufflé with the confectioners' sugar and bake for 2 to 3 minutes longer, until the sugar browns. Serve immediately, with the remaining warmed Apricot Sauce on the side.

▶ **If you beat the egg whites nicely and fold them in so as not to deflate them, a soufflé baked on a platter should rise a good 3 inches as it bakes. You can make the soufflé base 30 minutes or so in advance, leaving it in the saucepan and covering it with an upside-down bowl. The egg whites will suffer only a slight loss of puffing power.**

Apricot Sauce

Sauce á l'Abricot

MAKES ABOUT 3 CUPS

8 ounces dried apricots, rinsed and drained
½ cup water
½ cup dry vermouth
1 cinnamon stick or ¼ teaspoon ground cinnamon
½ lemon, quartered and seeded
½ cup granulated sugar, or more to taste
16 ounces canned apricot halves packed in water
⅛ teaspoon salt
1 to 2 teaspoons unsalted butter, softened (optional)

1 In a medium-sized saucepan, combine the dried apricots, water, and vermouth. Let soak for at least 1 hour, or overnight if the fruit is especially dry. (You may need to add another ¼ cup of water for longer soaking.)

2 Add the cinnamon stick and lemon to the pan of apricots, and bring to a simmer over medium heat. Cook for 20 minutes.

3 Stir in the sugar and the canned apricots, with their juices. Reduce the heat to low and cook, stirring frequently to prevent the sauce from scorching and sticking, for 20 to 30 minutes, or until thick and almost caramelized. Taste frequently, and add additional sugar, a tablespoonful at a time, if the sauce is too tart.

4 Transfer the apricot mixture to a blender or a food processor fitted with the metal blade. Blend until smooth. Blend in the butter, if using. Serve hot or cold.

▶ **This sauce can be made up to 1 week in advance, covered, and refrigerated. It can also be frozen for up to 3 months.**

▷ JULIA CHILD: **Apple Soufflé on a Platter with Apricot Sauce**

A Festive Cosmopolitan Dinner

*Burger of Fresh Foie Gras and Frisée Salad
with Cider Vinaigrette*
FOIE GRAS HACHÉ SUR SALADE FRISÉE AVEC VINAIGRETTE AU CIDRE

Squab With Cabbage and Mashed Potatoes
PIGEON AU CHOU ET PURÉE DE POMMES DE TERRE

Lemon Tart
TARTE CITRON

WINE SUGGESTIONS:

Syrah (*first course*)

California Merlot or Pomerol (*second course*)

California Sparkling Blanc de Blancs (*dessert*)

WHAT YOU CAN PREPARE AHEAD OF TIME

The night before: Clean the frisée for the Burger of Fresh Foie Gras. Wrap in damp paper towels and refrigerate.

Early in the day: Prepare and sauté the apples, porcini, and diced foie gras for the Burger of Fresh Foie Gras. Cover separately and refrigerate. Just before serving, reheat for about 5 minutes in a preheated 275 degress F. oven. Braise the cabbage for the Squab with Cabbage and Mashed Potatoes. Cover and refrigerate. Make the sauce for the Squab with Cabbage and Mashed Potatoes. Cover and refrigerate. Reheat in the top of a double boiler over simmering water. Prepare and bake the Lemon Tart. Just before the guests arrive, glaze under the preheated boiler.

In the afternoon: Make the Cider Vinaigrette for the Burger of Fresh Foie Gras. Make the sauce for the Burger of Fresh Foie Gras. Reheat in the top of a double boiler over simmering water.

I first met a young Christian Delouvrier when he was chef at the Maurice restaurant in New York City's Parker Meridien Hotel. As he prepared the recipes demonstrated at his first De Gustibus class, we were all overwhelmed by his use of lush ingredients in extraordinary ways. When he became chef at the acclaimed and stunning Les Célébrités, we asked him to come back and share some of his signature dishes with us. Again, he brought some crowd-pleasing showstoppers.

◁ Lemon Tart (recipe on page 47)

Burger of Fresh Foie Gras and Frisée Salad with Cider Vinaigrette

SERVES 6
PREPARATION TIME: ABOUT 25 MINUTES
COOKING TIME: ABOUT 45 MINUTES

Foie Gras Haché sur Salade Frisée avec Vinaigrette au Cidre

The traditional French combination of foie gras and apples is given a new twist. This very rich appetizer adds a festive note with its luxurious taste. This is Chef Delouvrier's tribute to "The Big Apple"!

VINAIGRETTE:

2 tablespoons cider vinegar
¼ cup plus 2 tablespoons light olive oil
Salt and freshly ground black pepper to taste
½ teaspoon minced fresh chervil
½ teaspoon minced fresh parsley
½ teaspoon minced fresh chives
½ teaspoon minced fresh tarragon

FOIE GRAS BURGERS:

2 cups chicken stock (see page 13)
6 small, tart apples, such as Granny Smith
2 tablespoons granulated sugar
2 to 3 tablespoons duck fat (see Note)
⅔ cup finely sliced fresh porcini mushrooms
3 ounces fresh foie gras, diced
2 tablespoons cider vinegar
6 slices fresh foie gras (about 2 ounces each), 3 to 4 inches wide and ½ inch thick
1 head frisée, trimmed, washed, and dried

1 Assemble the *mise en place* trays for this recipe (see page 9).

2 To make the vinaigrette, whisk together the vinegar and oil. Season to taste with salt and pepper. Stir in the minced fresh herbs. Set aside.

3 To make the foie gras burgers, in a small saucepan, bring the chicken stock to a boil over medium-high heat. Reduce the heat and simmer for about 20 minutes, or until reduced to ¾ cup. Remove from the heat and set aside.

4 Peel the apples. Trim each end, cutting crosswise through the center. Cut 2 large slices from each apple the same thickness as the foie gras slices. Core the slices and sprinkle with the sugar. Keep the slices together as pairs. Chop enough of the trimmings to equal 1 cup.

5 Preheat the oven to 400 degrees F.

CHRISTIAN DELOUVRIER: Burger of Fresh Foie Gras and Frisée Salad with Cider Vinaigrette

6 In a medium-sized, nonstick sauté pan, heat 1 tablespoon of the duck fat over medium heat. Keeping the apple pairs together, carefully lay them in the fat and sauté for 8 to 10 minutes, turning once, until tender and glazed. Remove from the pan and set aside.

7 Add another tablespoon of duck fat to the pan. Add the porcini and sauté for 5 minutes, or until crisp. Remove from the pan and set aside.

8 Add the diced foie gras to the pan. Sauté for 3 minutes, or until golden. Using a slotted spoon, transfer the foie gras to paper towels to drain.

9 If the pan seems dry, add 1 more tablespoon of duck fat and heat until hot. Add the reserved chopped apple trimmings and cook, stirring frequently, for about 4 minutes, until the apples begin to soften and release liquid. Stir in the vinegar and deglaze the pan, scraping up all the brown bits. Cook for 2 to 3 minutes, until the vinegar has evaporated. Stir in the reserved chicken stock. Strain the sauce through a chinois or other fine sieve into a small saucepan, pressing on the apples to extract all the liquid. Taste and season with salt and pepper. Cover and keep warm.

10 Place 1 slice of foie gras on the bottom half of each apple slice. Place an equal portion of porcini on top of the foie gras and top with the matching apple slice. Place on a nonstick, rimmed baking sheet and bake for about 3 minutes, until the foie gras is just heated through. Remove from the oven.

11 In a bowl, toss the frisée with the vinaigrette. Arrange equal portions of frisée on one side of each serving plate. Spoon the diced foie gras over the salad. Place the foie gras burger next to the salad, drizzle the sauce over the burger, and serve.

NOTE: The duck fat gives the sauce and foie gras a wonderful flavor. If you cannot find it at your butcher or a gourmet shop, substitute chicken fat or vegetable or olive oil.

▶ Frisée is also called curly endive. A head is about 3 ounces.

▶ Buy the best grade of foie gras available. The flavors are very intense in this appetizer.

Squab with Cabbage and Mashed Potatoes

SERVES 6
PREPARATION TIME: ABOUT 45 MINUTES
COOKING TIME: ABOUT 2 HOURS AND 30 MINUTES

Pigeon au Chou et Purée de Pommes de Terre

Squab is a lovely dish to serve in the autumn. The tender birds, served with white truffles, strike the perfect note after the elegant foie gras appetizer.

CABBAGE:

1 small head of green cabbage (about 2 pounds) cored, quartered, and separated into leaves
6 strips bacon
3 onions, chopped
2 tablespoons duck fat
Salt and freshly ground black pepper to taste

POTATOES:

6 large baking potatoes
6 tablespoons unsalted butter
1 tablespoon white truffle oil
Salt and freshly ground black pepper to taste
½ ounce white truffle, cut into fine julienne

SAUCE:

6 squab wings (see below)
3 onions, coarsely chopped
3 carrots, coarsely chopped
6 tablespoons dry white wine
4 sprigs fresh thyme
6 cloves garlic

SQUAB:

3 one-pound squabs, wings removed
3 sprigs fresh thyme
3 bay leaves
3 cloves garlic
3 tablespoons unsalted butter
Freshly grated white truffles

1 Preheat the oven to 400 degrees F. Assemble the *mise en place* trays for this recipe (see page 9).

2 To prepare the cabbage, blanch the leaves for 1 minute in enough lightly salted boiling water to cover. Drain.

3 Fry the bacon in an ovenproof skillet over medium-high heat until the fat is rendered. Drain and crumble the bacon. Set aside. Discard all but 2 tablespoons of fat.

4 Add the onions to the pan and cook in the bacon fat for 3 to 5 minutes, until just softened. Add the damp cabbage leaves. Set a piece of waxed or parchment paper directly on top of the cabbage. Cover the pan with a lid or aluminum foil. Braise in the oven for 10 to 12 minutes, until the cabbage is tender. Transfer the cooked cabbage and onions to a clean bowl, and set aside.

5 To prepare the potatoes, puncture each one with a fork and wrap in aluminum foil. Bake for about 1 hour, until fork tender. Trim about ¾ inch off each end of the potatoes. Cut the potatoes in half lengthwise and scoop out the flesh, taking care not to tear the skin. Leave a thin layer of potato flesh on the skins to strengthen them. Set the potato skins aside to cool.

6 Put the potato flesh in a saucepan over medium heat and add the butter and truffle oil. Mash with a fork until the butter is fully incorporated and the potatoes are smooth. Stir in the julienned truffles.

7 Using kitchen scissors, a small sharp knife, or a 2-inch cookie cutter, cut six 2-inch circles from the potato skins. Spoon small mounds of potato on the potato skin circles and set aside to keep warm.

8 To make the sauce, heat a heavy roasting pan or skillet over high heat. When hot, add the squab wings and cook, stirring, for 8 to 10 minutes, until juices are released and caramelized on the bottom of the pan. Add the onion, garlic, and carrots and cook for about 10 minutes, over medium heat, until the vegetables soften. Add the wine to deglaze the pan. Add enough water to cover the bones and the thyme. Raise the heat to high and reduce the liquid by one third. Strain through a fine sieve, pressing on the solids to extract liquid. Discard the solids and set the sauce aside to keep warm.

9 To roast the squabs, using a small sharp knife, remove the necks and the giblets. Rinse the squabs and pat dry.

10 Insert 1 sprig of thyme, 1 bay leaf, and 1 clove of garlic into the cavity of each squab. Season each one inside and out with salt and pepper. Truss the legs with kitchen twine. Rub the squabs with butter.

11 Set the squabs, breast side up, on a rack in a heavy roasting pan and roast for 30 minutes. Turn the squabs over and continue roasting for 30 minutes longer. Baste with the pan juices and turn the squabs breast side up again. Roast for about 15 minutes longer, until golden brown and the juices run clear when the flesh is pricked with the tip of a sharp knife.

12 Meanwhile, melt the duck fat in a large skillet. Add the reserved braised cabbage and cook over high heat for 3 to 4 minutes, until heated through. Drain and toss with the reserved crumbled bacon.

13 Lift each squab from the pan and remove the legs. Slice the meat from the breast.

14 Spoon equal amounts of cabbage on each plate. Top each with half the breast meat and 1 leg from a squab. Arrange the potato mounds around the cabbage. Spoon

sauce over the squab and sprinkle with grated truffles. Serve immediately.

As shown in the photograph on page 46, the Squab with Cabbage and Mashed Potatoes can be served with accompaniments that enhance the flavors of the dish such as asparagus, carrots, morels, and peas.

▶ **Squab may have to be special-ordered. If you cannot find it, substitute Rock Cornish Game Hens.**

▶ **While there is no substitute for the rich flavor of duck fat, use olive oil or vegetable oil if you cannot find it at your butcher or specialty store.**

Lemon Tart

SERVES 6
PREPARATION TIME: ABOUT 20 MINUTES
COOKING TIME: ABOUT 25 MINUTES
COOLING TIME: 1 TO 1½ HOURS

Tarte Citron

This is a perfectly sublime ending to a rich, complex dinner. Once assembled, the tart requires only a minute under the broiler and then an hour to set, making it a breeze to prepare.

½ pound frozen puff pastry, thawed
1 cup fresh lemon juice (about 6 lemons)
6 large eggs
5 large egg yolks
1¼ cups granulated sugar
15 tablespoons unsalted butter, cut into pieces

■ **Special Equipment: 9-inch tart pan with removable bottom; pastry weights, dried beans, or rice**

1 Preheat the oven to 400 degrees F. Assemble the *mise en place* trays for this recipe (see page 9).

2 On a lightly floured surface, roll out the pastry about ⅛ inch thick into a circle approximately 12 inches round. Transfer the pastry to a 9-inch tart pan with a removable bottom. Gently fit the pastry into the pan, and trim off any excess. Prick the bottom of the pastry all over with a fork. Line the pastry with aluminum foil and spread pastry

weights, dried beans, or rice over the foil. Bake for 15 minutes, or until lightly browned. Remove from the oven. Lift off the foil and weights and set on a wire rack to cool.

3 Preheat the broiler.

4 In the top half of a double boiler, combine the lemon juice, eggs, egg yolks, and sugar. Set over simmering water. Using a hand-held electric mixer, beat for 8 to 10 minutes, or until the mixture is very thick and clings to the beater.

5 Remove from the heat. Using a whisk, whisk in the butter, a little at a time. Pour the custard into the partially baked pastry shell.

6 Place under the broiler for 1 minute, or until the top is glazed. Let sit at room temperature for 1 to 1½ hours, until the filling is cooled and set, before serving.

▶ **To extract as much juice as possible, roll the lemons on the countertop several times, exerting a small amount of pressure. If you wrap the halved lemon in cheesecloth before squeezing it, no pits or pulp will get in the juice (this only works for hand-squeezed lemons).**

A Taste of Provence

Mediterranean Seafood Soup
L'AïGO

Braised Lamb Shanks with Dried Mediterranean Fruits
JARRET D'AGNEAU AUX FRUITS DE BRANCONNIER

Chocolate Tarte with Orange Salad
TARTE SABLÉE AU CHOCOLAT AVEC SALADE D'ORANGE

WINE SUGGESTIONS:

Rosé de Provence, Gavi, or Pinot Grigio (*first course*)

Full-Bodied Pinot Noir or lighter Zinfandel (*second course*)

Vintage Character Port (*dessert*)

Jean-Michel Diot was one of our best surprises. I had expected Jacques Chibois, executive chef of the Royal Grey in Cannes and consultant at New York's Peninsula Hotel, to be part of one of our French series. At the last moment, he had an emergency in France and couldn't come. "Don't worry," said Chef Chibois, "I'll send my chef from the Peninsula. He trained with me and is terrific!" What he didn't tell me was that his terrific chef had only been in New York for six weeks, did not speak a word of English, and had never taught a cooking class.

After some anxiety, the class took place and this terrific chef, Jean-Michel Diot, received a standing ovation from the students. His food reflected all of the flavors and colors of the South of France, he smiled a lot, and his sous-chef was a great translator. It was one of our most exciting classes.

Jean-Michel subsequently learned English, opened three restaurants in New York City, and is now considered one of the city's leading chefs.

◁ Braised Lamb Shanks with Dried Mediterranean Fruits (recipe on page 51)

WHAT YOU CAN PREPARE AHEAD OF TIME

Up to 1 week ahead: Make the pastry for the Chocolate Tart. Fit it into the pan, wrap tightly in aluminum foil, and freeze. Thaw at room temperature before baking. (Thawing will take between 30 minutes and 1 hour, depending on the heat of the day.)

Up to 3 days ahead: Marinate the lamb shanks and reduce and strain the braising liquid for the Braised Lamb. Combine the meat and liquid, cover, and refrigerate. Reheat in the oven with the fennel mixture.

Up to 2 days ahead: Dice the dried fruits for the Braised Lamb. Cover tightly and refrigerate.

The day before: Prepare the orange juice and zest for the Braised Lamb. Cover and refrigerate.

The night before: Prepare all the vegetables for the Mediterranean Seafood Soup. Cover and refrigerate.

Early in the day: Prepare the lobster for the Mediterranean Seafood Soup. Cover and refrigerate. Cut the fennel and apples for the Braised Lamb into julienne. Toss separately with fresh lemon juice, cover, and refrigerate. Prepare the Orange Salad for the Chocolate Tart.

Mediterranean Seafood Soup

L'Aïgo

This soup is redolent of the sea and of the intensely pure flavors of the South of France. It would make a great Sunday-night supper along with a crisp white wine, crisp baguettes, and crisp greens! The soup begins with water flavored with garlic, and builds from there. No need to make stock. The scallops most readily available are sea scallops, the larger type which must be halved or quartered before using in this recipe. Substitute sliced green beans for fava beans, if necessary.

8 cloves garlic
3 cups water
1 one-pound lobster
½ cup white wine
3 shallots, diced
12 mussels, well scrubbed and bearded
12 clams, well scrubbed
1 four-ounce zucchini
1 four-ounce yellow squash
4 ounces fresh fava beans, shelled (about ⅓ cup, shelled)
2 cups diced, trimmed fennel bulb (about 1¼ pound bulb)
4 ounces sea scallops, rinsed
1 teaspoon tomato paste
¼ cup plus 1 tablespoon olive oil
¾ pound very ripe tomatoes, cored, peeled, seeded, and diced
2 tablespoons chopped fresh basil
1 tablespoon chopped fresh tarragon
4 tablespoons unsalted butter
Salt and freshly ground black pepper to taste
6 large fresh oysters, shucked

1 Assemble the *mise en place* trays for this recipe (see page 9).

2 Peel the garlic. Crush 2 of the cloves, and set aside.

3 In a medium-sized saucepan, combine the remaining 6 garlic cloves and the water. Bring to a simmer over medium-high heat.

4 Meanwhile, plunge a knife into the lobster just behind the head to kill it instantly. Cut off the claws.

5 Add the lobster body and claws to the garlic water, return to the boil, cover, and cook for about 8 minutes.

JEAN-MICHEL DIOT: Mediterranean Seafood Soup

Remove the lobster from the water and set aside to cool. Continue boiling the liquid for about 15 minutes, or until reduced to 2 cups. Set aside.

6 In a medium-sized saucepan, combine the white wine, shallots, and reserved crushed garlic. Bring to a simmer. Add the mussels and clams, cover, and cook for 2 minutes, until the shells open. Using a slotted spoon, remove the shellfish, discarding any that do not open. Reserve the shellfish cooking liquid. Open the shells and remove the meat. Discard shells.

7 Remove the meat from the tail and claws of the lobster and cut it into ¼-inch-thick slices.

8 Trim the ends of the zucchini and yellow squash and cut in half lengthwise. Put each half, cut side down, on a work surface and cut into slices about ⅛ inch thick. Set aside.

9 Blanch the fava beans in boiling water to cover for 1 minute. Drain and refresh under cold running water. Peel. Set aside in a small bowl.

10 Blanch the fennel in boiling water to cover for 1 minute. Drain and refresh under cold running water. Add to the bowl with the fava beans.

11 Place the scallops on a flat surface and, using a sharp knife, cut horizontally into halves or quarters to make slices about ¼ inch thick. Refrigerate.

12 Combine the reserved garlic water, the shellfish cooking liquid, and the tomato paste in a blender or a food processor fitted with the metal blade. Blend until smooth. With the motor running, add the olive oil, a little at a time. Transfer to a large saucepan. Add the squash slices and bring to a boil over high heat. Cover and simmer for about 6 minutes, or until the squash is just tender but not mushy.

13 Add the diced tomatoes, fava beans, and fennel to the saucepan. Stir in the basil and tarragon. Stir in the butter, a little at a time. Season to taste with salt and pepper.

14 Reduce the heat and add the mussels, clams, scallops, and oysters. Cook for 1 minute, or until the oysters curl around the edges. Add the lobster meat and cook for 1 minute more, until just heated through. Serve in warm soup bowls.

Braised Lamb Shanks with Dried Mediterranean Fruits

SERVES 6
PREPARATION TIME: ABOUT 1 HOUR AND 20 MINUTES
COOKING TIME: ABOUT 3 HOURS AND 15 MINUTES
MARINATING TIME: 12 HOURS

Jarret d'Agneau aux Fruits de Branconnier

Perhaps the Arab traders left their mark on the South of France with the flavors of this dish, redolent with cumin, coriander seed, and dried fruits. It is great for entertaining since the dish is even better after it has rested for a day or two.

1 small leek, trimmed
½ bunch fresh flat-leaf parsley
5 to 6 sprigs fresh sage
1 sprig fresh thyme
1 bay leaf
6 lamb shanks
3 carrots, peeled and diced
6 cloves garlic, crushed
3 shallots, diced
¼ cup plus 2 tablespoons olive oil
1 tablespoon cumin seed
1 teaspoon coriander seed
1 tablespoon coarse salt, or to taste
1 tablespoon cracked black pepper, or to taste
4 cups dry white wine
2 tablespoons all-purpose flour
3 ripe tomatoes, cored, quartered, and seeded
3 cups water
6 dried figs
6 dried apricots
6 dried dates
2 tablespoons raisins
1 bunch fresh mint, washed and dried
3 tart apples, such as Granny Smith
6 fennel bulbs, trimmed, cored, and cut into ⅛-inch-thick slices
Grated zest and juice of 1 orange

1 Assemble the *mise en place* trays for this recipe (see page 9).

2 Make a bouquet garni by tying the leek, parsley, sage, thyme, and bay leaf together with a piece of kitchen twine. In a Dutch oven, combine the lamb shanks, carrots, garlic, shallots, 2 tablespoons of the olive oil, the cumin seed, coriander seed, salt, pepper, and the bouquet garni. Add the wine and stir to mix. Cover and place in the refrigerator to marinate for 12 hours.

3 Preheat the oven to 300 degrees F.

4 Remove the lamb shanks from the marinade. Strain the

marinade, reserving the liquid. Reserve the vegetables and bouquet garni separately.

5 In the Dutch oven, heat 2 tablespoons of the olive oil over medium-high heat. Add the lamb shanks and sear, turning frequently, for 10 to 15 minutes, or until well browned. Transfer to paper towels to drain.

6 Add the marinated vegetables to the pot and cook for 5 to 6 minutes, until they have just begun to release their liquid. Transfer to a bowl with a slotted spoon, and set aside.

7 Using a wooden spoon, stir the flour into the juices remaining in the pot. Cook, stirring constantly, for about 3 minutes, or until the flour is golden brown.

8 Return the lamb shanks and vegetables to the pot. Add the tomatoes, the reserved marinade, and the bouquet garni. Increase the heat to high and bring to a boil. Reduce the heat and simmer for about 20 minutes, or until the liquid is reduced by half.

9 Stir in 2 cups of the water. Cover and transfer to the oven. Cook for about 2 hours or until the meat is very tender.

10 Meanwhile, dice the figs, apricots, dates, and raisins.

Cut the mint leaves into fine julienne and combine with the diced fruit. Set aside.

11 About 45 minutes before the meat is ready, peel and core the apples and cut into 1/8-inch-thick slices.

12 In a large ovenproof sauté pan, heat the remaining 2 tablespoons of oil over medium heat. Add the fennel and sauté for about 5 minutes, just until it begins to brown. Stir in the apples and orange zest and juice. Stir in the remaining 1 cup of water, cover, and cook in the oven for 30 minutes.

13 Arrange the fennel mixture in the center of a large platter. Place the lamb shanks on top. Cover with a piece of aluminum foil to keep warm.

14 Place the Dutch oven over high heat, bring the liquid to a boil for about 5 minutes, until reduced and slightly thickened. Skim off any fat that rises to the surface. Strain into a saucepan and stir in the dried fruit mixture. Simmer for 4 to 5 minutes, until fruit softens. Season to taste with salt and pepper.

15 Ladle some of the sauce over the top of the lamb. Serve with the remaining sauce on the side.

Chocolate Tart with Orange Salad

SERVES 6
PREPARATION TIME: ABOUT 30 MINUTES
COOKING TIME: ABOUT 1 HOUR AND 15 MINUTES
CHILLING AND COOLING TIME: ABOUT 3 HOURS AND 25 MINUTES

Tarte Sablée au Chocolat avec Salade d'Orange

A chocolate dessert as seductive as this one tastes even better when served with an orange salad for a slightly acidic accent and refreshing note.

1¾ cups unsalted butter, at room temperature
2 cups granulated sugar
5 large eggs
¼ teaspoon salt
1½ cups all-purpose flour
12 ounces bittersweet chocolate
¼ cup cornstarch
2 large egg yolks
1 tablespoon confectioners' sugar
Orange Salad (recipe follows)

■ Special Equipment: 10-inch tart pan with removable bottom. Pastry weights, dried beans, or rice.

1 Assemble the *mise en place* trays for this recipe (see page 9).

2 In a large bowl, using an electric mixer set on medium-high speed, beat 12 tablespoons of the butter, ½ cup of the granulated sugar, 1 of the eggs, and the salt for 3 to 4 minutes, until light colored and thick. Reduce the speed to medium-low and slowly add the flour, about ½ cup at a time, being careful not to overmix the dough. Form the dough into a flattened ball, wrap in plastic, and refrigerate for at least 2 hours.

3 Preheat the oven to 350 degrees F.

4 Lay a large piece of waxed paper on a lightly floured surface and dust the paper with flour. Put the chilled dough on the paper and sprinkle lightly with flour. Lay a second

52

JEAN-MICHEL DIOT: **Chocolate Tart with Orange Salad**

sheet of waxed paper over the dough, and roll it out to a 13-inch circle. Carefully transfer the paper-wrapped pastry to the refrigerator and chill for about 15 minutes.

5 Peel off the top piece of waxed paper and carefully transfer the chilled dough, paper side up, to a 10-inch tart pan with a removable bottom. Gently lift off the remaining piece of waxed paper, fit the pastry into the pan, and trim off any excess. Prick the bottom of the pastry all over with a fork. Line the pastry shell with aluminum foil, and spread pastry weights, dried beans, or rice over the foil. Bake for 10 to 15 minutes, until lightly browned. Lift out the weights and foil and and set on a wire rack to cool. Do not turn off the oven.

6 In the top half of a double boiler, melt the chocolate over barely simmering water. Beat in the remaining 1 cup

of butter, a little at a time, until well incorporated. Remove from the heat.

7 In a large bowl, using an electric mixer set on medium-high speed, beat the egg yolks, the remaining 4 eggs, and 1½ cups of sugar for 3 to 4 minutes, until light and creamy. Whisk in the cornstarch until well blended. Slowly whisk in the chocolate mixture.

8 Scrape the mixture into the partially baked pastry shell. Bake for about 1 hour, or until the center is set. Transfer to a wire rack to cool for at least 1 hour before serving.

9 Just before serving, dust the tart with confectioners' sugar. Cut into wedges and serve with the Orange Salad on the side.

ORANGE SALAD
Salade d'Orange

MAKES ABOUT 4 CUPS

8 oranges
2 tablespoons bitter orange marmalade
3 tablespoons granulated sugar

1 With a small, sharp knife remove the colored peel from 4 of the oranges, being careful to avoid any bitter white pith. Cut the peel into fine julienne.

2 Blanch the julienne in boiling water for 15 seconds. Drain and refresh under cold running water. Pat dry and set aside.

3 Working over a bowl, cut all the peel and pith from all 8 oranges, letting any juices drip into the bowl. Slice between the membranes to free each segment, dropping the segments into the bowl. Squeeze the juice from the membranes and discard them.

4 Add the marmalade, reserved zest, and the sugar to the orange segments. Stir to combine. Cover and refrigerate until ready to serve.

A TYPICAL FRENCH MEAL

Creamy Carrot Soup
SOUPE DE CAROTTES À L'ANETH

Fillet of Beef with Horseradish Sauce
FILET DE BOEUF À LA FICELLE AVEC SAUCE AU RAIFORT

Thin Apple Tart
TARTE AUX POMMES À LA MINUTE

WINE SUGGESTIONS:

Chardonnay (*first course*)

Red Bordeaux, St. Estèphe or Pauillac (*second course*)

Calvados (*dessert*)

WHAT YOU CAN PREPARE AHEAD OF TIME

Up to 1 week ahead: Prepare the Chicken Stock (if making your own). Prepare the Beef Stock (if making your own).

Up to 2 days ahead: Make the Carrot Soup. Cover and refrigerate.

The day before: Make the Horseradish Sauce. Cover and refrigerate.

Early in the day: Prepare all the vegetables for the Fillet of Beef. Place in a sealed plastic bag and refrigerate. Tie the beef with the kitchen twine. Cover and refrigerate. Bake the Thin Apple Tart. Before serving, heat in a pre-heated 300 degree F. oven for 5 minutes.

It was a thrill and an honor to have Pierre Franey teach in the De Gustibus kitchen. For many of us, Pierre is the essence of the charming French chef. He enchanted us with his stories of his early cooking days and amazed us with tales of his experiences at *The New York Times.*

Pierre's first visits to De Gustibus were in our "formative years," and he was one of the first "real" French chefs to teach a class. None of us had ever seen such order around the stove. I don't know what was more impressive—his organizational skills or his fastidious presentation. We had never witnessed what was to Chef Franey perfectly normal, well-learned culinary practice. More than any other chef, he taught us how important the basic cooking habits are in accomplishing great meals. Furthermore, Pierre made good cooking really accessible. Not only is he a great French chef, he is a warm human being who enjoys cooking for family and friends.

◁ Creamy Carrot Soup (recipe on page 56)

Creamy Carrot Soup

Soupe de Carottes à l'Aneth

This simple soup has great taste, it can be made in advance, and it can be served hot or cold. What more could a home cook ask?

2 tablespoons unsalted butter
1 cup minced onions
5 cups sliced carrots
Salt and freshly ground black pepper to taste
4 cups Chicken Stock (see page 13)
½ cup ricotta cheese
2 tablespoons port wine
2 tablespoons chopped fresh dill

1 Assemble the *mise en place* trays for this recipe (see page 9).

2 In a medium-sized saucepan, melt the butter over medium heat. Add the onions and cook, stirring occasionally, for 4 to 5 minutes, until softened.

3 Stir in the carrots and season to taste with salt and pepper. Add the chicken stock and bring to a boil. Reduce the heat and simmer, partially covered, for 30 minutes. Strain, reserving the liquid.

4 Transfer the carrot mixture to a blender or a food processor fitted with the metal blade. Add the ricotta and 1 cup of the reserved liquid. Process until smooth. Scrape back into the saucepan and add the remaining liquid.

5 Return the soup to the heat and bring to a boil. Remove from the heat and stir in the port and dill. Serve hot. Alternately, allow to cool just to warm room temperature, cover, and refrigerate for at least 4 hours until well chilled. Stir in the port and dill just before serving cold.

Fillet of Beef with Horseradish Sauce

Filet de Boeuf à la Ficelle avec Sauce au Raifort

Although, for this menu, the meat should be cooked just before serving, all the other components of the recipe can easily be prepared in advance. However, the beef is also terrific cold, so the dish could be cooked early in the day, especially during warm weather, when cold meals are always welcome.

1¼ pounds center-cut fillet of beef
4 cups Beef Stock (see page 14)
1 bay leaf
2 sprigs fresh parsley
3 sprigs fresh thyme, chopped, or ½ teaspoon dried thyme
Salt and freshly ground black pepper to taste
1 large leek, white part only, washed and cut into julienne (about 2 cups)
1 large parsnip, peeled and cut into julienne (about 2 cups)
2 carrots, peeled and cut into julienne (about 2 cups)
1 small onion, halved and finely sliced (about ½ cup)
Horseradish Sauce (recipe follows)

1 Assemble the *mise en place* trays for this recipe (see page 9).

2 Carefully tie the meat lengthwise and crosswise with kitchen twine, leaving a long end of string as a handle to facilitate removing the meat from the cooking liquid.

3 In a large, heavy saucepan or flame-proof casserole with lid, combine the stock, bay leaf, parsley, thyme, and salt and pepper to taste. Add the beef, leaving the length of string outside the pan.

4 Cover the pan, bring the stock to a simmer over medium-high heat, and cook for exactly 5 minutes. Immediately add the leeks, parsnips, carrots, and onion and stir to distribute them. Cover and simmer for exactly 7 minutes. Remove from the heat and let stand, covered, for 5 minutes.

▷ PIERRE FRANEY: Fillet of Beef with Horseradish Sauce

56

5 Remove the beef from the pan and cut into thin slices (no more than ½-inch thick). Arrange on a warm platter. Spoon the vegetables around the meat and spoon a little of the liquid over all. Serve with the Horseradish Sauce passed on the side.

▶ If you cannot buy a center-cut fillet but instead buy an end of the fillet, trim the tapering ends before cooking.

▶ You can, of course, lift the meat from the pan with tongs rather than using the string as a handle, but do not pierce it with a fork.

▶ Substitute drained white bottled horseradish for grated horseradish in the horseradish sauce, if necessary.

HORSERADISH SAUCE
Sauce au Raifort

MAKES ABOUT ½ CUP

½ cup sour cream
2 tablespoons freshly grated horseradish, or to taste
1 teaspoon white wine vinegar
⅛ teaspoon Tabasco
Salt and freshly ground black pepper to taste

In a bowl, combine the sour cream, 2 tablespoons of horseradish, the vinegar, and Tabasco. Stir to blend. Season to taste with salt and pepper, and add more horseradish, if desired.

SERVES 6
PREPARATION TIME: ABOUT 20 MINUTES
COOKING TIME: ABOUT 20 MINUTES

Thin Apple Tart

Tarte aux Pommes à la Minute

This is one of my favorite French desserts. It is so simple and the apple flavor just shines!

1½ cups all-purpose flour, chilled
6 tablespoons unsalted butter, chilled and cut into pieces
3 tablespoons plus 2 teaspoons granulated sugar
¼ cup cold water
3 large, tart apples, such as Granny Smith, peeled, cored, and thinly sliced
1 tablespoon unsalted butter, melted

■ Special Equipment: dark-colored, 12-inch pie pan or pizza pan

1 Preheat the oven to 450 degrees F. Assemble the *mise en place* trays for this recipe (see page 9).

2 Put the flour, butter, and 2 teaspoons of the sugar in a food processor fitted with the metal blade. With the motor running, slowly add the water through the feed tube and process for about 1 minute, until the dough forms a ball.

3 Transfer the dough to a lightly floured surface and roll out into a circle about 13 inches in diameter. Press into a 12-inch shallow black steel or aluminum pie pan or pizza

◁ PIERRE FRANEY: Thin Apple Tart

pan about ½ inch deep. Trim any dough that rises up the side of the pan to make a flat round.

4 Sprinkle the dough with 1 tablespoon of the sugar. Arrange the apple slices neatly in an overlapping circular pattern on the dough, starting from the center and forming concentric rings. The center will rise to a slight peak, but it will flatten during baking. If there is space in the middle, fill it with some chopped apple. Sprinkle the apples with the remaining 2 tablespoons of sugar.

5 Bake for about 20 minutes, until the apples are lightly browned and soft and the sugar has begun to brown.

6 Remove the tart from the oven, and turn the oven setting to broil.

7 When the broiler is hot, place the tart under it for 1 minute to caramelize the sugar on top. The rims of the apple slices should be well browned, but watch carefully so that the pastry does not get too brown. Remove from the broiler and brush the top with the melted butter. Cut into wedges and serve hot.

▶ **Cut the apples as thin as possible. They should be as uniformly shaped as possible for even cooking. You can cut them into either circles or half-moon shapes.**

COLONIAL FRANCE—
FRENCH FOOD WITH A TOUCH OF ASIA

*Sautéed Shrimp with Marinated Spaghetti Squash
and Curry-Cilantro Vinaigrette*
POÊLE DE CREVETTES ET SPAGHETTI DE COURGES AU CURRY

Spicy Broth of Bass and Halibut Flavored with Lovage
CONSOMMÉ ÉPICÉ DE FLÉTANS ET BAR DE L'ATLANTIQUE
AVEC LIVÈCHES ("CÉLERI BÂTARD")

Chilled Soup of Santa Rosa Plums Flavored with Vanilla
SOUPE GLACÉE AUX PRUNES PARFUMÉE DE VANILLE

WINE SUGGESTIONS:

Dry Riesling (German or Washington State)

Premier Cru Chablis

WHAT YOU CAN PREPARE AHEAD OF TIME

Up to 1 week ahead: Prepare the Fish Stock (if making your own). Prepare the Vegetable Stock (if making your own).

The day before: Make the Chilled Soup of Santa Rosa Plums. Cover and refrigerate.

Early in the day: Prepare all the components for the Sautéed Shrimp except the shrimp. Store separately, covered, in the refrigerator. Prepare the Curry-Cilantro Vinaigrette, but do not add the cilantro until just before serving. Cover and store at room temperature. Make the pistachio-coated ice cream balls for the Chilled Soup of Santa Rosa Plums. Set on a baking sheet in a single layer and freeze until ready to use.

Gray Kunz is a dazzling chef. He grew up in Switzerland, where he trained with Freddy Girardet, one of the world's great cooking gurus, before spending a number of years cooking in Asia. Recently, he brought his genius to New York. Now chef at the acclaimed restaurant Lespinasse at the Hotel St. Regis, Gray Kunz continues to receive accolades for his refined flavors.

Chef Kunz has an eye for detail both in the kitchen and on the plate. His marriage of zesty Asian ingredients with classic French techniques has opened new horizons for the De Gustibus students. Totally interested in our classroom enthusiasms, Gray has been a great supporter of our students and a great friend to all of us.

◁ Chilled Soup of Santa Rosa Plums Flavored with Vanilla (recipe on page 65)

Sautéed Shrimp with Marinated Spaghetti Squash and Curry-Cilantro Vinaigrette

SERVES 6
PREPARATION TIME: ABOUT 25 MINUTES
COOKING TIME: ABOUT 1 HOUR

Poêle de Crevettes et Spaghetti de Courges au Curry

A perfectly light but flavor-packed first course. The Asian flavors add a refreshing zing to the otherwise sweetly bland spaghetti squash. The squash mixture is so delicious that you will want to serve it alone as a tasty salad or side dish.

1 two-to-two-and-one-half-pound spaghetti squash
1 small candy cane beet or regular beet, cooked, peeled, and thinly sliced
1/3 cup thinly sliced firm but ripe papaya
1/4 cup thinly sliced hothouse cucumber
Grated zest of 1 lime
1 tablespoon minced fresh ginger
1 1/2 teaspoons minced fresh parsley
3 tablespoons rice wine vinegar
2 1/2 tablespoons corn oil
1 teaspoon granulated sugar
1/4 teaspoon salt
1/4 teaspoon freshly ground white pepper
6 jumbo shrimp, peeled and deveined
1 ounce mesclun greens or other delicate leaf salad mix
Curry-Cilantro Vinaigrette (recipe follows)

1 Preheat the oven to 375 degrees F. Assemble the *mise en place* trays for this recipe (see page 9).

2 Prick the squash with a fork in a few places to prevent it from bursting. Put it in a shallow baking dish and bake for 1 hour, or until it depresses easily when gently pressed. Remove from the oven and immediately cut lengthwise in half. Allow to cool for about 10 minutes.

3 Remove and discard the seeds from the squash. Using a kitchen fork, lift the strands of "spaghetti" from each half. Measure out 2 cups of squash and place in a large bowl. Let squash cool. Reserve any remaining squash for another use.

4 Add the beet, papaya, cucumber, lime zest, ginger, and parsley to the squash, and toss well.

5 In a small bowl, whisk together the vinegar, 1 1/2 table-spoons of the oil, the sugar, salt, and white pepper. Pour over the squash mixture and toss. Taste and adjust the seasoning. Set aside.

6 In a small sauté pan, heat the remaining 1 tablespoon of oil over medium-high heat. Add the shrimp and sauté for 2 minutes, or until the shrimp turns pink and opaque. Remove from the heat.

7 Mound the squash mixture in the center of 6 plates. Surround with the mesclun. Put the shrimp on top of the squash mixture, drizzle the Curry-Cilantro Vinaigrette over all, and serve immediately.

▶ Select a papaya that is just ripe. It should be firm but slightly yielding. If it is too green, the flesh will be unpleasantly hard; if too ripe, it will not hold up well in the salad.

▶ If papayas are unavailable, you could use a firm but ripe mango.

CURRY-CILANTRO VINAIGRETTE
MAKES ABOUT 1/3 CUP

3 tablespoons vegetable oil
1 1/2 tablespoons white wine vinegar
3/4 teaspoon curry powder
1 1/2 tablespoons Vegetable Stock (see page 15) or water
1/2 teaspoon fresh lemon juice, or to taste
Salt and freshly ground black pepper to taste
Granulated sugar to taste
2 tablespoons chopped fresh cilantro

1 In a small bowl, whisk together the oil, vinegar, and curry powder. Add the stock. Season to taste with lemon juice, salt, pepper, and a pinch of sugar. Add more sugar, if desired.

2 Just before serving, stir in the cilantro.

▷ GRAY KUNZ: Sautéed Shrimp with Marinated Spaghetti Squash and Curry-Cilantro Vinaigrette

Spicy Broth of Bass and Halibut Flavored with Lovage

SERVES 6
PREPARATION TIME: ABOUT 25 MINUTES
COOKING TIME: ABOUT 35 MINUTES

Consommé Épicé de Flétans et Bar de l'Atlantique avec Livèches ("céleri bâtard")

This is a perfectly simple fish course that can easily become a main course for a light lunch.

½ pound fresh black sea bass fillet, skinned, trimmed, and cut into ½-inch cubes

½ pound fresh halibut fillet, skinned, trimmed, and cut into ½-inch cubes

Salt and freshly ground black pepper to taste

3 leaves lovage, chopped, or ¼ cup chopped celery leaves

1 teaspoon vegetable oil, or more if necessary

4 cups Fish Stock (see page 15)

4 tablespoons unsalted butter, cut into pieces

2½ tablespoons minced shallots

½ teaspoon minced garlic

Cayenne pepper to taste

½ cup cored, peeled, seeded, and diced tomatoes

¼ cup diced green bell pepper

⅓ cup thinly sliced leeks

■ Special Equipment: mortar and pestle

1 Assemble the *mise en place* trays for this recipe (see page 9).

2 Put the lovage in a mortar and add the vegetable oil. Using a pestle, grind into a paste, adding additional oil if necessary for a pesto-like consistency. Alternatively, mince the chopped lovage leaves and mix them with the oil in a small bowl, pressing down and grinding with the edge of a wooden spoon until the mixture forms a paste-like consistency.

3 In a medium-sized saucepan, bring the stock to a boil over medium-high heat. Reduce the heat to low. Using a whisk, beat the butter into the stock, a piece at a time, until emulsified. Do not add the next piece until the one before is incorporated. Stir in the shallots and garlic. Season to taste with salt and black pepper and cayenne. Bring the mixture to a gentle boil.

GRAY KUNZ: Spicy Broth of Bass and Halibut Flavored with Lovage

4 Season the fish with salt and pepper to taste.

5 Add the tomato, pepper, and leeks to the pan and return to a gentle boil. Add the fish. As soon as the liquid returns to a gentle boil, remove the pan from the heat and stir in the lovage mixture. Taste and adjust the seasoning, if necessary.

6 Ladle the fish and broth into 6 warm, shallow soup bowls. Serve immediately.

▶Lovage, called céleri bâtard, or "false celery," in France because its flavor and aroma are similar to celery, is extremely potent. Use it sparingly. Lovage is easy to grow in a vegetable garden. It is sold at greengrocers and farm markets. As indicated in the recipe, you can substitute celery leaves for lovage if necessary.

▶If you like the flavor of lovage, make small amounts of lovage "pesto" as described in Step 2, cover and refrigerate. Use it to flavor stews, soups, salads, or sauces or to season roasted or grilled meats.

▶If you cannot find black sea bass, substitute any firm-fleshed white fish or use all halibut. Recommended substitutes include grouper, striped sea bass, and snapper.

Chilled Soup of Santa Rosa Plums Flavored with Vanilla

SERVES 6
PREPARATION TIME: ABOUT 20 MINUTES
COOKING TIME: ABOUT 1 HOUR
CHILLING TIME: AT LEAST 4 HOURS

Soupe Glacée aux Prunes Parfumée de Vanille

This dessert is best made in the summer, when plums are at their most succulent. For fewer calories and no fat, eliminate the ice cream. The idea of serving "soup" for dessert is a delicious one you may not have tried.

2½ pounds overripe red plums, preferably Santa Rosa, washed
½ cup plus 1 tablespoon granulated sugar, or to taste
1 vanilla bean, split in half lengthwise
Juice of 1 lemon, or more to taste
10 cups water
Dash of Mirabelle eau-de-vie or other plum-flavored liqueur
1 cup chopped, toasted pistachio nuts (see page 13)
1 pint high-quality vanilla ice cream

1 Assemble the *mise en place* trays for this recipe (see page 9).

2 Cut 6 silver dollar-sized slices from the sides of 2 or 3 plums. Chop the remaining plum flesh, discarding the pits.

3 In a medium-sized saucepan, combine the sliced and chopped plums, ½ cup of the sugar, the vanilla bean, lemon juice, and water. Bring to a simmer over medium heat. Reduce the heat to low and simmer, uncovered, for 20 minutes.

4 Using a slotted spoon, carefully transfer 6 plum slices to a plate and sprinkle with the remaining 1 tablespoon of sugar. Set aside. Continue simmering the chopped plum mixture, uncovered, for about 40 minutes more.

5 Strain the chopped plum mixture through a fine sieve into a glass or ceramic bowl, pushing against the solids to extract all the juice. Discard the solids. Taste, and add a little more sugar, if necessary. Cover and refrigerate for about 4 hours, or until well chilled.

6 Just before serving, stir the eau-de-vie or plum liqueur into the soup. Taste, and add lemon juice, if necessary. Ladle the soup into 6 well-chilled, shallow soup bowls.

7 Place the pistachios in a shallow bowl. Scoop out 6 small balls of ice cream and roll each one in the pistachios. Place an ice cream ball in the center of each bowl of soup, lay a sugared plum slice on top, and serve immediately. If not using ice cream, simply garnish the soup with the plum slices.

▶When a recipe calls for overripe plums, select those that feel heavy and juicy and are very "giving" when pressed. Avoid any that are still firm—or that show signs of spoilage.

TALKING TURKEY IN THE FRENCH MANNER

Lettuce Soup
SOUPE DE LAITUES

Scallopine of Turkey Breast with Morel and Cognac Sauce
ESCALOPE DE JEUNE DINDE AUX MORILLES AVEC SAUCE AU COGNAC

Fricassee of Turkey and Brown Rice
FRICASÉE DE DINDE AU RIZ BRUN

Baked Apples
POMMES BONNE FEMME

WINE SUGGESTIONS:

Champagne (*first course*)

California Pinot Noir or Red Burgundy (*second course*)

Syrah or Merlot (*third course*)

Calvados (*dessert*)

WHAT YOU CAN PREPARE AHEAD OF TIME

Up to 1 week ahead: Prepare the Turkey or Chicken Stock (if making your own).

Up to 1 day ahead: Make the Lettuce Soup, but if serving hot, do not add the lettuce. Cool, cover, and refrigerate, and reheat just before serving, adding the shredded lettuce. If serving cold, add the lettuce, cool, cover, and refrigerate. Prepare the Fricassee of Turkey, but do not add the peas and parsley. Cool, cover, and refrigerate. Reheat in a preheated 300 degree F. oven for 30 minutes, adding additional liquid if necessary, and stir in the peas and parsley just before serving.

Early in the day: Prepare the components of the Scallopine of Turkey Breast. Cover separately and refrigerate.

Jacques Pépin is the Rachmaninoff of chefs. When he first came to De Gustibus, we had never seen a chef so adroit, skillful, and speedy with a knife. Jacques's technical skills were amazing.

Over the years, he has done many demonstration classes for us, so we have come to understand his philosophy of cooking. He has taught us how to cook efficiently, that we must never waste anything, and that the expensive product is not always the best. When Jacques demonstrated the following menu, it was not as easy to get "turkey parts" as it is now. His menu utilizes his practical and economic approach to ingredients by providing separate recipes for different parts of the turkey. Early in our history, Jacques set the standard for excellence that we strive to maintain at De Gustibus.

◁ Baked Apples (recipe on page 71)

Lettuce Soup

Soupe de Laitues

Not only is this soup easy to make—it is delicately beautiful to look at. A French favorite not often seen in the American kitchen, lettuce soup, which has a potato base, can be served hot or cold.

5 tablespoons unsalted butter
1 cup chopped onions
1 cup chopped leeks, washed and drained
8 cups Turkey or Chicken Stock (see page 13)
4 cups diced, peeled baking potatoes
1 teaspoon salt
2 small heads Boston lettuce, leaves separated, washed, and dried

1 Assemble the *mise en place* trays for this recipe (see page 9).

2 In a large saucepan, heat 3 tablespoons of the butter over medium heat. Add the onions and leeks and sauté for about 2 minutes. Add the stock, potatoes, and salt and bring to a boil. Reduce the heat to low and simmer, partially covered, for about 40 minutes, until the potatoes are very tender.

3 Transfer the mixture to a blender or a food processor fitted with the metal blade, and blend until smooth. You may have to do this in batches to avoid overflow. Return the soup to the pan and set over low heat.

4 Stack the lettuce leaves a few at a time, roll them up cigar fashion, and slice into chiffonade (thin strips).

5 In a medium-sized saucepan, heat the remaining 2 tablespoons of butter. Add the chiffonade and sauté for about 3 minutes, until wilted. Stir into the soup. Adjust seasoning to taste.

6 Ladle the soup into 6 warm soup bowls and serve immediately.

JACQUES PÉPIN: Lettuce Soup

Scallopine of Turkey Breast with Morel and Cognac Sauce

SERVES 6
PREPARATION TIME: ABOUT 35 MINUTES
COOKING TIME: ABOUT 50 MINUTES
SOAKING TIME (MUSHROOMS ONLY): ABOUT 30 MINUTES

Escalope de Jeune Dinde aux Morilles avec Sauce au Cognac

Scallopine of turkey breast is much less expensive than veal but just as elegant with the morels and Cognac—a typically practical French solution!

3 ounces dried morels
4 cups lukewarm water
6 slices turkey breast, each about 6 ounces and about ³⁄₈-inch thick
1½ teaspoons salt, or more to taste
1 teaspoon freshly ground black pepper, or more to taste
2 to 3 tablespoons unsalted butter
½ cup chopped shallots
1 tablespoon finely chopped garlic
2 tablespoons Cognac
1½ cups heavy cream
1 teaspoon potato starch or cornstarch (optional)
Few drops of fresh lemon juice

1 Assemble the *mise en place* trays for this recipe (see page 9).

2 In a bowl, combine the morels and water. Let the mushrooms soak for about 30 minutes, until reconstituted and softened.

3 Drain the morels, reserving the soaking liquid. Remove any dirty or sandy stems. Cut in half lengthwise, or quarter if very large.

4 Strain the reserved soaking liquid through a fine sieve lined with paper towels into a small saucepan. Bring to a boil over medium-high heat. Reduce the heat to low and simmer for about 30 minutes, until reduced to 1 cup.

5 Preheat the oven to 175 degrees F.

6 Season the turkey slices on both sides with the salt and pepper.

7 In a large skillet, melt 1 tablespoon of the butter over medium-high heat. When hot, add 2 of the turkey slices. Cook for about 2 minutes, turning once. Arrange in a single layer in a large shallow ovenproof dish, and keep warm in the oven. Cook the remaining turkey slices in the same way, adding more butter as needed.

8 When all the turkey is cooked, add the shallots and garlic to the skillet. Reduce the heat to medium and cook for about 30 seconds. Add the Cognac to the skillet. Carefully ignite the Cognac and flambé; it will extinguish almost immediately.

9 Add the reduced mushroom liquid and the cream. Bring to a boil, stirring to scrape up any browned bits. Stir in the juices that have accumulated around the turkey slices. Strain the sauce into a clean saucepan. Stir in the morels, place over medium heat, and bring to a boil. Reduce the heat and simmer for about 3 minutes. Season to taste with

JACQUES PÉPIN: Scallopine of Turkey Breast with Morel and Cognac Sauce

salt and pepper. If the sauce seems thin, dissolve the potato starch or cornstarch in 1 tablespoon of cold water and whisk it into the simmering sauce so that it thickens enough to thinly coat the back of a spoon. Stir in the lemon juice.

10 Arrange the turkey slices on a warm serving platter and spoon the sauce and mushrooms over them. Serve immediately.

▶ You can slice the turkey from a whole turkey breast half, or you can buy packaged turkey cutlets, which are usually cut about ⅜ inch thick.

▶ Whenever you work with raw poultry, be sure to wash the work surfaces and utensils, as well as your hands, with warm, soapy water before proceeding with another task. This prevents the spread of salmonella bacteria.

▶ Even cooked turkey should not be left at room temperature for longer than necessary. Refrigerate any leftovers as soon as the main course is over.

Fricassee of Turkey and Brown Rice

SERVES 6
PREPARATION TIME: ABOUT 30 MINUTES
COOKING TIME: 1 HOUR AND 45 MINUTES TO 2 HOURS

Fricassée de Dinde au Riz Brun

This is a great dish with which you can feed a crowd. It is inexpensive, nutritious, and easy to make ahead of time. And, if there are any leftovers, it's even better when reheated. Either this or the Scallopine of Turkey Breast can be served as a main course. Or you can serve both.

2 turkey legs and 2 turkey wings (about 5 pounds)
3 tablespoons unsalted butter
1½ pounds yellow onions, chopped
4 ounces loose-packed sun-dried tomatoes, chopped
3 tablespoons chopped garlic
1 teaspoon ground cumin
½ teaspoon red pepper flakes
3 bay leaves
2 teaspoons salt
1 teaspoon freshly ground black pepper
1½ cups brown rice
5 cups water
1 cup tiny peas, blanched in boiling water for 1 minute
¼ cup chopped fresh parsley

1 Assemble the *mise en place* trays for this recipe (see page 9).

2 Using a cleaver, cut each turkey leg into 5 pieces and each wing into 2 pieces. Remove any tough tendons.

JACQUES PÉPIN: Fricassee of Turkey and Brown Rice

70

3 In a large skillet or Dutch oven, melt the butter over medium heat. Add the turkey pieces and sear, turning frequently, for about 15 minutes, or until well browned on all sides.

4 Add the onions and cook for about 10 minutes until the onions soften. Add the sun-dried tomatoes, garlic, cumin, hot pepper flakes, bay leaves, and salt and pepper. Stir in the rice and water, increase the heat, and bring to a boil. Cover, reduce the heat, and simmer for about 1 hour and

10 minutes, or until all the liquid has been absorbed and the turkey meat and rice are very tender.

5 Remove from the heat, and remove the bay leaves. Stir in the peas and parsley, and serve immediately.

▶ **Fresh peas are best for this recipe, but you may use high-quality frozen or canned tiny peas.**

▶ **You can have the butcher chop the turkey into pieces. Ask him to remove the tendons at the same time.**

Baked Apples

SERVES 6
PREPARATION TIME: ABOUT 15 MINUTES
COOKING TIME: ABOUT 1 HOUR

Pommes Bonne Femme

A simple dessert straight from the kitchen of "la grand'mère."

6 large, tart apples, such as Russet, Granny Smith, or Pippin, cored
⅓ cup apricot jam
⅓ cup pure maple syrup
3 tablespoons unsalted butter, cut into 6 pieces

1 Preheat the oven to 375 degrees F. Assemble the *mise en place* trays for this recipe (see page 9).

2 With the point of a knife, cut an incision about ⅛ inch to ½ inch wide through the skin all around each apple, about a third of the way down from the stem end. As the apples cook, the flesh expands and the tops of the apples will lift up like a lid above this cut. Without this scoring, the apples will burst.

3 Stand the apples upright in a gratin dish or other attractive ovenproof dish. Coat the apples with the apricot jam and maple syrup and dot them with the butter. Bake for 30 minutes.

4 Baste the apples with the cooking juices and bake for 30 to 40 minutes longer, or until the apples are plump, brown, and soft to the touch. Serve warm.

▶ **If you prepare the apples early in the day, bake them while you are dining so that they are served hot from the oven.**

▶ **Delicious served with a slice of pound cake or with sour cream or ice cream.**

A PERFECT MARRIAGE

Roasted Eggplant Roulade with Oregano and Marinated Goat Cheese
PAUPIETTE D'AUBERGINES AU FROMAGE DE CHÈVRE MARINÉ A L'ORIGAN

Lamb Stew with Fall Fruits and Vegetables
LE SAUTÉ D'AGNEAU AUX ARTICHAUTS, POMMES, ET HARICOTS NOIRS

Crème Brûlée Le Cirque

WINE SUGGESTIONS:

Sauvignon Blanc or Pinot Blanc (*first course*)

Châteauneuf-du-Pape (*second course*)

Aged Tawny Port (*dessert*)

WHAT YOU CAN PREPARE AHEAD OF TIME

Up to 1 week ahead: Prepare the Lamb Stock (if making your own).

Up to 3 days ahead: Prepare the brown sugar for the Crème Brûlée.

Up to 1 day ahead: Prepare the Roasted Eggplant Roulade. Prepare the lamb cubes for the Lamb Stew. Cover and refrigerate. Soak the black beans for the Lamb Stew.

Early in the day: Prepare and cook the artichokes, potatoes, and black beans for the Lamb Stew. Cover and refrigerate. Prepare the diced tomatoes and minced herbs for the Lamb Stew. Cover separately and refrigerate. Bake the Crème Brûlée. Cool, cover, and refrigerate without the sugar. Caramelize the sugar on the top just before serving.

It is very hard to view your husband objectively. It is even harder when you run cooking classes and he is a well-known French chef whose meals, whether at home or at work, are always delicious! I have learned more about French food from Alain than from anyone else, simply because I see him cook it every day.

Although known for his knowledge of French culinary techniques and his intimacy with the classic French repertoire, Alain is a very modern chef. When he teaches, he makes himself totally accessible. He seems to know what diners demand in a contemporary menu and he has a flexibility about cooking that can accommodate their needs. He also has a quiet patience with his students and me! Needless to add, in my eyes, he is a great chef —and an even greater husband!

◁ Roasted Eggplant Roulade with Oregano and Marinated Goat Cheese (recipe on page 74)

Roasted Eggplant Roulade with Oregano and Marinaed Goat Cheese

SERVES 6
PREPARATION TIME: ABOUT 45 MINUTES
COOKING TIME: ABOUT 15 MINUTES
MARINATING TIME: ABOUT 1 HOUR
CHILLING TIME: AT LEAST 8 HOURS

Paupiette d'Aubergines au Fromage de Chèvre Mariné a l'Origan

This recipe has lots of components, but each one is easy to prepare. An even greater boon for home entertaining is that the roulade should be made the day before serving. Without the radicchio and tomato garnish, it would also make a terrific, simple hors d'oeuvre.

1 ten-ounce goat cheese log, sliced into 5 equal portions
1 tablespoon plus ½ teaspoon minced garlic
3 tablespoons chopped fresh oregano
½ cup plus 1 teaspoon olive oil
Freshly ground black pepper to taste
1 large eggplant (about 1½ pounds), trimmed and cut lengthwise into ⅛-inch-thick slices
Salt to taste
1 pound fresh spinach leaves, washed and dried
1 roasted red bell pepper, peeled (see page 12), seeded, and diced
6 ripe plum tomatoes
3 tablespoons chopped fresh basil
Juice of ½ lemon
12 small radicchio leaves, washed and dried
12 small celery leaves, washed and dried

1 Assemble the *mise en place* trays for this recipe (see page 9).

2 In a bowl, combine 2 tablespoons of the olive oil, 1 teaspoon of the garlic, and the oregano. Season to taste with pepper. Add the goat cheese and let marinate for 1 hour at room temperature.

3 Preheat the oven to 450 degrees F.

4 Lay the eggplant slices in a large colander so that they overlap slightly. Sprinkle them with a little salt. Set aside for 10 minutes. Rinse and immediately pat dry.

5 Brush a baking sheet with 1 tablespoon of the olive oil. Lay the eggplant slices on the baking sheet. Brush with 2 tablespoons of the olive oil. Bake for 5 to 10 minutes, until the eggplant begins to brown. Set aside.

6 In a medium-sized sauté pan, heat 2 tablespoons of the olive oil over medium heat. Add the spinach, 1 teaspoon of the garlic and salt and pepper to taste. Cook, stirring, for about 5 to 6 minutes, until wilted, tossing the spinach with tongs to ensure all the leaves wilt. Remove from the heat.

7 In a medium bowl, combine the diced red pepper, 1 tablespoon of the olive oil, and 1 teaspoon of the garlic. Season to taste with salt and pepper. Stir in the spinach.

8 Drain the goat cheese well. Add to the red pepper mixture and mash to make a smooth, spreadable mixture. Check the seasoning.

9 Line a 12 x 18-inch baking sheet with plastic wrap. Arrange the eggplant slices, overlapping, to cover the plastic, leaving a 1-inch border all around. Spread the spinach and cheese mixture evenly over the eggplant. Lift the plastic wrap along the long side nearest you and gently roll the eggplant into a roulade. Twist the plastic wrap at each end to tighten it and form an even jelly-roll shape. Leaving the roulade on the baking sheet, chill for at least 8 hours.

10 Blanch the tomatoes in boiling water for 10 seconds. Drain and refresh in ice water. Peel and seed the tomatoes and cut into small dice.

11 About an hour before serving, in a medium bowl, combine the diced tomatoes, the remaining 1 teaspoon of olive oil, and the remaining ½ teaspoon of garlic. Add the chopped basil, lemon juice, and salt and pepper to taste. Set aside.

12 Remove the roulade from the refrigerator. Do not remove the plastic. Using a sharp knife dipped in hot water for 1 second and then wiped dry, cut 18 half-inch slices from the roulade, dipping the knife in the hot water and drying it between each slice. Arrange 3 slices in a triangle pattern on each of 6 chilled serving plates, removing the plastic.

13 Place 2 radicchio leaves in the center of each triangle. Spoon about 2 tablespoons of the tomato mixture onto the radicchio leaves, and arrange 2 celery leaves on top of the tomatoes. Serve immediately.

Lamb Stew with Fall Fruits and Vegetables

SERVES 6
PREPARATION TIME: ABOUT 2 HOURS
COOKING TIME: ABOUT 4 HOURS AND 30 MINUTES
SOAKING TIME (BEANS ONLY): AT LEAST 6 HOURS

Le Sauté d'Agneau aux Artichauts, Pommes, et Haricots Noirs

Complex flavors combine to make a beautiful and very aromatic fall casserole. The lamb could be served alone, with just its delicious sauce, accompanied by rice or noodles, a crisp salad, and a bottle of young red wine.

¼ pound dried black beans, soaked in cold water for 6 hours
1 tablespoon unsalted butter
2 firm tart apples, such as Jonathan or McIntosh, peeled, cored, and sliced
1 tablespoon all-purpose flour
7 cups cold water
Juice of 1 lemon
Salt
1 lemon, halved
4 ½-pound artichokes
4 red-skinned potatoes (about 1 pound)
¼ cup olive oil
4 pounds boneless stewing lamb, trimmed and cut into 2-inch cubes
2 carrots, peeled and diced
2 ribs celery, diced
3 large onions, chopped
1 whole bulb garlic, cloves separated, peeled, and chopped
Freshly ground black pepper to taste
1 cup Lamb Stock (see page 14), or water
8 ounces button mushrooms, wiped clean, trimmed, and quartered
8 ounces pleurotte or oyster mushrooms, wiped clean, trimmed, and halved
1 cup diced, peeled, and seeded tomatoes
1 tablespoon minced fresh flat-leaf parsley
1 teaspoon minced fresh thyme
1 teaspoon minced fresh oregano

1 Assemble the *mise en place* trays for this recipe (see page 9).

2 Drain the beans and place in a large saucepan with enough fresh cold water to cover by at least 2 inches. Bring to boil over high heat, reduce the heat, and simmer for 1½ hours, or until soft.

3 Meanwhile, in a medium-sized sauté pan, melt the butter over medium heat. Add the apples and sauté for 6 to 8 minutes, until golden brown. Remove from the heat.

4 Drain the beans, reserving ½ cup of the cooking liquid. In a blender or a food processor fitted with the metal blade, combine the beans, sautéed apples, and reserved bean-cooking liquid. Blend for about 1 minute, until smooth. (Bits of black bean will still be visible.) Transfer to a bowl and set aside.

5 In a large saucepan, beat together the flour and 1 cup of the water. Stir in 3 more cups of water, the lemon juice, and 1½ teaspoons of salt. Bring to a boil over medium-high heat. Immediately remove from the heat and set aside to cool for about 15 minutes.(This mixture, known as a blanc, will be used to cook the artichokes and insure that they will not discolor.)

6 Cut the stem off 1 of the artichokes. Bend the leaves back and snap them off, leaving the edible leaf bottoms attached to the base. Continue to remove the leaves until you reach the soft crown of leaves in the center. Cut off this core of leaves. Using a small, sharp knife, trim the base evenly to remove all the greenish parts and create a perfect round. To keep the artichoke from discoloring, rub the cut surfaces frequently with the halved lemon as you work. Drop the artichoke into the blanc, and repeat with the remaining artichokes. If the artichokes are not completely covered, add additional water, as necessary.

7 When all the artichokes are trimmed, put the pan over medium-high heat and bring to a boil. Reduce the heat and simmer for 30 minutes, or until the artichoke bottoms are tender when pierced with a knife.

8 Drain the artichokes well and rinse under cold running water. Pat dry with paper towels. Scoop out the chokes (fuzzy interior) with a teaspoon and discard. Pat dry. Cut the artichoke bottoms into quarters and set aside.

9 Cut the potatoes lengthwise. Using a very sharp knife, trim the potatoes into perfectly uniform ovals (to resemble large olives), by turning them in your fingers as you cut away the flesh.

75

10 Put the potatoes in a medium-sized saucepan, with enough cold water to cover. Add salt to taste and a few drops of lemon juice. Cover and bring to a boil over medium-high heat. Reduce the heat and simmer for 8 to 10 minutes, or until just tender. Drain and set aside.

11 In a very large, deep sauté pan or Dutch oven, heat 1 tablespoon of the olive oil over medium-high heat. Sauté the meat, in 2 or 3 batches, for about 10 minutes, until browned. Do not crowd the pan. Spoon off liquid as it accumulates in the pan. When all the meat is browned, set the lamb aside.

12 Pour off the fat in the pan. Add 1 cup of water and deglaze over medium heat, stirring to scrape up any brown bits sticking to the bottom. Cook for 8 to 10 minutes, stirring, until most of the liquid has evaporated. Return the lamb to the pan.

13 Heat 1 tablespoon of the olive oil in a medium-sized sauté pan over medium-high heat. Add the carrots, celery, and onions and sauté for 10 to 12 minutes, until browned. Add the chopped garlic and sauté for 1 minute longer.

14 Add the stock and 2 more cups of water to the meat, increase the heat, and bring to a boil. Add the sautéed vegetables, reduce the heat to low, cover, and simmer for 1½ hours, or until the lamb is very tender.

15 Skim the fat from the top of the stew. Using a slotted spoon, transfer the meat to a platter and set aside.

16 Strain the cooking liquid and vegetables through a fine sieve into a large saucepan, pushing against the solids to extract all the liquid. Discard the solids. Stir in the bean and apple purée. Add the lamb and keep warm over very low heat.

17 Meanwhile, in a medium-sized saucepan, heat the remaining 2 tablespoons of olive oil over medium heat. Add the mushrooms and sauté for 8 minutes, or until tender. Stir in the artichokes and potatoes to just heat through. Check the seasonings.

18 Spoon the lamb with the sauce into the center of a serving platter. Arrange the vegetable mixture around it. Sprinkle the tomatoes over the vegetables. Sprinkle with the minced parsley, thyme, and oregano, and serve immediately.

ALAIN SAILHAC:
**Lamb Stew with Fall
Fruits and Vegetables**

Crème Brûlée Le Cirque

This is the ultimate crème brûlée, the most classic of all French desserts. There are now many Americanized versions, but, in my opinion, this is the one and only, rich and delicious "burnt cream."

½ cup packed light brown sugar
4 cups heavy cream
1 vanilla bean, split
½ cup plus 2 tablespoons granulated sugar
6 large egg yolks

■ **Special Equipment: Shallow 8-ounce oval ramekins**

1 Spread the brown sugar on a small baking sheet. Place, uncovered, in a dry spot for at least 24 hours, or until the sugar is quite dry. Push through a fine sieve. Set aside.

2 Assemble the *mise en place* trays for this recipe (see page 9).

3 Preheat the oven to 350 degrees F.

4 In a medium-sized saucepan, heat the cream and vanilla bean over medium heat for 3 minutes, or until just warm.

5 In a bowl, whisk together the granulated sugar and egg yolks. When well blended, whisk in the cream. Strain through a fine sieve into a bowl.

6 Divide the mixture among 6 eight-ounce shallow oval ramekins. Place in a shallow roasting pan and add enough hot water to come halfway up the side of the ramekins. Bake for about 30 minutes, or until set and a knife inserted in the center comes out clean. The custards will still be soft; do not overbake.

7 Transfer the custards to wire racks to cool for at least 30 minutes.

8 Preheat the broiler.

9 Spoon the brown sugar into a fine sieve and sprinkle evenly over the tops of the custards. Broil for about 15 seconds to melt and burn the sugar topping. Watch carefully to prevent charring. Serve immediately.

ALAIN SAILHAC: Crème Brûlée *Le Cirque*

▶ **Many chefs use a blow torch or a crème brûlée iron to make the brittle burnt sugar topping. Here, the broiler is equally effective because the sugar is already so dry.**

A TRADITIONAL ALSATIAN DINNER

Onion Tart
TARTE AUX OIGNONS

Stuffed Breast of Veal
POITRINE DE VEAU

Potato Pancakes
GALETTES AUX POMMES DE TERRE

Chocolate Mousse
MOUSSE AU CHOCOLAT

WINE SUGGESTIONS:

Alsatian Riesling or Sparkling Wine (*first course*)

Red Villages-level Burgundy or Chianti Classico (*second course*)

Ruby Port (*dessert*)

WHAT YOU CAN PREPARE AHEAD OF TIME

Up to 1 week ahead: Make the pastry for the Onion Tart. Line tart pan with the pastry, wrap tightly, and freeze. Thaw before filling.

Up to 2 days ahead: Stuff and cook the Breast of Veal. Skim the pan juices. Cool quickly, and refrigerate the veal and juices in the roasting pan. Reheat for 30 minutes in a preheated 300 degree F. oven before serving.

Early in the day: Chop the onions for the Onion Tart. Cover and refrigerate. Make the stuffing for the Breast of Veal, if not already stuffed and baked. Cover and refrigerate. As a safety precaution, do not stuff the veal until ready to cook. Make the batter for the Potato Pancakes. Cook just before serving. Make the Chocolate Mousse.

A ndré Soltner of Lutèce is an inspiration to all home cooks. He is the only chef ever to orchestrate an entire De Gustibus class by himself, showing us firsthand that it is quite possible to cook a grand meal without a fully staffed kitchen. He never ceases to amaze me.

Chef Soltner always plays to a full house at De Gustibus. And what a maestro! Every audience has been mesmerized both by his cooking and by his stories of the road he took to become one of the world's superstar chefs. An afternoon with André is always one of the highlights of the season's classes. He leaves us all eagerly anticipating his next visit.

◁ Stuffed Breast of Veal and Potato Pancakes (recipe on page 81)

Onion Tart

Tarte aux Oignons

This is a classic French recipe and one that has remained on the menu at Lutèce since the day the restaurant opened. Proof that one can never get too much of a good thing.

2 cups all-purpose flour
Salt
4 tablespoons chilled, unsalted butter
½ cup cold water
2 tablespons lard
3 large yellow onions, chopped
½ cup heavy cream
1 large egg
Freshly ground black pepper to taste
Freshly grated nutmeg to taste

■ Special Equipment: 8-inch tart pan with removable bottom

1 Assemble the *mise en place* trays for this recipe (see page 9).

2 In a medium-sized bowl, combine the flour and 1 teaspoon of salt. With your fingertips or a pastry blender, quickly blend in the butter until the mixture resembles coarse meal. Stir in the water and quickly mix to form a soft dough. Do not overmix, or the pastry will be tough. Shape the pastry into a ball and flatten slightly. Wrap in plastic and chill for at least 1 hour.

3 Preheat the oven to 375 degrees F.

4 In a large sauté pan, melt the lard over medium heat. Add the onions and sauté for 10 to 15 minutes, or until lightly browned. Transfer to a bowl.

5 In a small bowl, beat cream and egg together. Add to the onions, stirring to combine. Season to taste with salt, pepper, and nutmeg. Set aside.

6 On a lightly floured surface, roll out the pastry to a circle about 10 inches in diameter. Transfer the pastry to an 8-inch tart pan with a removable bottom. Gently fit the pastry into the pan, and trim off any excess pastry.

ANDRÉ SOLTNER: Onion Tart

7 Spoon the onion filling into the pastry shell. Bake for 25 to 35 minutes, or until well browned. Cut into wedges and serve hot.

▶ Lard imparts a distinct flavor to the onions, and Chef Soltner recommends using it. However, you can substitute olive oil or butter.

▶ Served at room temperature, the tart makes a great hors d'oeuvre for a cocktail party.

Stuffed Breast of Veal

Poitrine de Veau

From Chef Soltner: "In the small town of Thann, which is the town I come from in Alsace, every year there is a Poitrine de Veau Festival. The festival is held on a weekend in late spring when the weather is warm. The whole town comes and people from the region all around.

"A giant tent is set up. There is music and dancing, which goes on long into the night. The town orders huge amounts of poitrine de veau, and it is sold by the slice. All the money goes to the town — for the fire department, or for something like that. Of course, with all that poitrine de veau, the people drink a large amount of cold beer, and also a great deal of Alsatian white wine. Everyone has a good time. Some people say that this dish was brought to Alsace by the Romans. It could be. But the festival is a local invention."

STUFFING:

1 tablespoon unsalted butter
1 small onion, sliced
¾ cup milk
2 cups cubes of crustless, home-style white bread
8 ounces boneless stewing veal, cut into 1-inch cubes (from neck or shoulder)
8 ounces pork butt, cut into 1-inch cubes
2 medium eggs
1 tablespoon chopped fresh parsley
2 tablespoons Cognac
Salt and freshly ground black pepper to taste

VEAL:

3 pounds boned breast of veal, trimmed of fat
Salt and freshly ground black pepper
1 tablespoon unsalted butter
1 tablespoon peanut oil
1 cup chopped carrots
1 cup diced onions
½ cup diced celery
1 cup dry white wine
½ cup water

■ Special Equipment: Trussing needle and kitchen twine

1 Assemble the *mise en place* trays for this recipe (see page 9).

2 To make the stuffing, in a large sauté pan, melt the butter over medium heat. Add the onion and sauté for about 5 minutes, until softened. Remove from the heat and set aside.

3 In a medium-sized saucepan, warm the milk over low heat. Remove from the heat, and add the bread cubes, and soak for about 3 minutes.

4 Remove the bread from the milk and squeeze it gently to remove most, but not all, of the milk. Put the cubes in a large bowl and stir in the onions.

5 Process the cubed veal and pork, in batches, in a food processor fitted with a metal blade or a blender until just chopped. Do not overprocess. Add the chopped meat to the bread and onions and stir to combine. Stir in the eggs, parsley, and Cognac and season to taste with salt and pepper.

6 Preheat the oven to 325 degrees F.

7 To prepare the veal, cut a pocket in the side of the breast of veal, being careful not to cut all the way through the meat. Carefully fill the pocket with the stuffing, making sure the pocket is well packed. Using a trussing needle and kitchen twine, sew the pocket closed. Generously season the stuffed breast all over with salt and pepper.

8 In a roasting pan, heat the butter and oil over medium heat. Add the meat and sear for about 12 minutes, or until well browned on all sides. Add the carrots, onions, and celery. Season to taste with salt and pepper.

9 Roast for 1 hour, turning the meat once during roasting, and basting occasionally with the pan juices.

10 Reduce the oven temperature to 300 degrees F. and add the wine and water to the roasting pan. Cover the meat with a sheet of buttered parchment paper or a loose lid of buttered aluminum foil and roast for about 1 hour and 15 minutes longer, basting frequently.

11 Remove the pan from the oven and transfer the meat to a cutting board. Cover loosely with aluminum foil and allow to rest for 15 minutes.

12 Skim the fat from the pan juices. Taste and adjust the seasoning with salt and pepper, if necessary.

13 Remove the string from the meat and discard. Cut the meat into ½-inch-thick slices. Arrange on a serving platter and spoon the pan juices around the meat. Serve immediately.

▶ Sewing up a stuffed breast of veal is a simple task. Trussing needles, which resemble oversized sewing needles, are sold in kitchenware shops. Use them as you would any needle, but your stitches need only be tidy enough to hold the filling in place. They are removed after the veal is cooked.

▶ Breast of veal is not an everyday item in the butcher shop, and you will probably have to special order it a few days before the party. Ask the butcher to remove the bone (it should weigh about 3 pounds after boning) and, if you like, to cut the pocket for you.

▶ A small, sharp knife is the best tool for making the pocket in the veal. Insert the blade and cut a slit along the side of the meat. Do not let the knife cut all the way through the meat. Then insert the blade in the slit again and wiggle it up and down to open the pocket a little.

▶ This stuffing would be good with chicken, turkey, and boned pork too.

▶ If the stuffing is made earlier in the day, keep it refrigerated. Do not stuff the veal until ready to cook, as bacteria can grow.

Potato Pancakes

SERVES 6
PREPARATION TIME: ABOUT 30 MINUTES
COOKING TIME: ABOUT 40 MINUTES

Galettes aux Pommes de Terre

French potato pancakes! Light as a feather and so delicious. Galettes can be eaten "as is," or served with meat dishes to absorb sauces and gravies.

1 pound baking potatoes, peeled and cubed
Salt to taste
¼ cup milk
3 tablespoons all-purpose flour
2 large eggs
3 large egg whites
¼ cup heavy cream
¼ cup clarified butter (see page 12)

■ Special Equipment: potato ricer

1 Assemble the *mise en place* trays for this recipe (see page 9).

2 In a medium-sized pan, combine the potatoes, salt to taste, and enough cold water to cover. Bring to a boil over medium-high heat, reduce the heat, and simmer for about 15 minutes, or until soft. Drain well. Put through a potato ricer into a bowl.

3 Add the milk to the riced potatoes and beat until smooth. Stir in the flour until blended. Beat in the eggs, one at a time, and then beat in the egg whites. Stir in the cream. Do not overwork the mixture.

4 Preheat the oven to 175 degrees F.

5 Heat about 1 tablespoon of the clarified butter in a medium-sized nonstick sauté pan. Drop the batter into the pan by the ladleful. Cook the pancakes for about 2 minutes on each side, or until lightly brown and set. Transfer to a baking sheet and keep warm in the oven. Continue cooking the pancakes, adding more butter as needed. The batter makes 15 to 18 pancakes. Sprinkle with salt and serve hot.

▶ The French word *galette* translates roughly to mean "cake-shaped."

Chocolate Mousse

Mousse au Chocolat

Here it is—the sublime. Nobody can resist Chef Solt-ner's chocolate mousse.

1¾ cups granulated sugar
2 tablespoons corn syrup
½ cup water
4 large eggs, separated
½ teaspoon cream of tartar
½ teaspoon instant coffee granules
1 teaspoon dark rum
3 tablespoons unsalted butter, melted and cooled
8 ounces bittersweet chocolate, chopped
1 large egg
3 cups heavy cream

■ **Special Equipment:** candy thermometer; pastry bag fitted with a star tip

1 Assemble the *mise en place* trays for this recipe (see page 9).

2 Combine ¾ cup of the sugar, 1 tablespoon of the corn syrup, and ¼ cup of the water in a small, heavy saucepan. Bring to a boil over high heat and boil for 15 minutes, or until the syrup reaches 248 degrees F. on a candy thermometer.

3 Just before syrup is ready, using an electric mixer fitted with a wire whisk, whip the 4 egg whites until foamy. Beat in the cream of tartar.

4 Gradually drizzle the hot syrup into the egg whites, beating as you pour. Then continue beating until the mixture has cooled to room temperature and forms stiff peaks. Set aside.

5 Melt the chocolate in the top half of a double boiler set over barely simmering water, stirring occasionally until smooth. Remove from the heat and set aside.

6 Combine the remaining cup of sugar, 1 tablespoon corn syrup, and ¼ cup water in a small heavy saucepan. Bring to a boil over high heat and boil for 15 minutes, or until the syrup reaches 248 degrees F. on a candy thermometer.

7 Just before the syrup is ready, whisk the egg yolks and egg in a large bowl.

8 Gradually drizzle the hot syrup into the beaten yolks, beating as you pour. Then continue beating until the mixture has cooled to room temperature.

9 Dissolve the instant coffee in the rum. Stir into the egg whites and then stir in the melted butter.

10 Fold the melted chocolate into the egg yolk mixture. Gently fold this mixture into the egg whites just until the egg whites are completely incorporated. The egg whites will lighten the mixture; overfolding will cause it to deflate slightly.

11 Whip the cream until stiff and fold into the chocolate mixture. Spoon one cup of mousse into a pastry bag fitted with a star tip and refrigerate. Spoon the remaining mousse into a serving bowl, cover with plastic wrap, and refrigerate for at least 2 hours.

12 When ready to serve, pipe a design on top of the mousse with the reserved mousse in the pastry bag.

ANDRÉ SOLTNER: **Chocolate Mousse**

A VEGETABLE TASTING

Napoléon of Roquefort and Boursin
MILLEFEUILLE DE ROQUEFORT ET BOURSIN

Wild Mushroom Crêpes
GÂTEAU DE CRÊPES AUX CHAMPIGNONS SAUVAGES

Beet Tartare
TARTARE DE BETTERAVES ROUGES

Passion Fruit Club with Strawberries
"CLUB" DE FRUITS DE LA PASSION AUX FRAISES

WINE SUGGESTIONS:

Champagne

WHAT YOU CAN PREPARE AHEAD OF TIME

Up to 3 days ahead: Prepare the Beet Tartare. Cover and refrigerate. Bring to room temperature before serving. Bake the cookies for the Passion Fruit Club.

Up to 2 days ahead: Prepare the duxelles for the Wild Mushroom Crêpes. Cover and refrigerate. Prepare the crêpes for the Wild Mushroom Crêpes. Cover and refrigerate.

Up to 4 hours ahead: Assemble the Napoléon.

Jean-Georges Vongerichten is probably the most versatile French chef we have ever hosted at De Gustibus. Each of his classes have been unique and unpredictable. He is so filled with creative concepts and stimulating recipes that we await each visit with enormous anticipation, truly wondering, "What's cooking?"

Chef Vongerichten has presented us with classic French cuisine, bistro meals, a taste of Thailand, and, our biggest surprise, a meal made entirely of vegetables.

All of us remember Jean-Georges's first De Gustibus demonstration not for the Thai food, but for the ties. He had brought five cooks to assist him, including two of his brothers. None of them had ever done a cooking class and all were absolutely delighted with an audience and a photographer. Although ready to face home cooks, however, they did not feel appropriately dressed for a formal portrait. So, since we were at Macy's, they all went downstairs to the shops. These chic French chefs returned wearing new, fashionably narrow ties, ready to pose for the camera.

◁ Wild Mushroom Crêpes (recipe on page 87)

Napoléon of Roquefort and Boursin

Millefeuille de Roquefort et Boursin

This delicious cheese dish can be served either as an appetizer or as a cheese course after the meal. Best of all, it can be cooked in advance and reheated just before serving.

3 sheets phyllo dough, thawed
4 tablespoons unsalted butter, melted
4 ounces Roquefort cheese
4 ounces Boursin cheese
½ cup heavy cream, softly whipped
1 tablespoon chopped fresh chives
½ teaspoon Cognac
Salt and freshly ground black pepper to taste

■ Special Equipment: pastry bag with a plain tip (optional)

1 Preheat the oven to 450 degrees F. Assemble the *mise en place* trays for this recipe (see page 9).

2 Stack the phyllo sheets on a baking sheet, brushing each one with some of the melted butter, making sure to brush all the way to the edges of the phyllo. Trim the stack into a 12-inch square. Discard the trimmings. Bake for 3 to 4 minutes, until golden brown. Allow to cool for at least 20 minutes.

3 In a blender or a food processor fitted with the metal blade, blend the Roquefort and Boursin cheese until smooth. Scrape into a bowl and gently but thoroughly fold in the whipped cream. Fold in the chives and Cognac, and season to taste with salt and pepper.

4 Using a very sharp knife, cut off a 3 x 12-inch strip from the cooled phyllo stack. Set aside.

5 Spoon the cheese mixture into a pastry bag fitted with a plain tip, and pipe evenly over the baked rectangle, making sure the piped lines touch each other. Or, gently spread the cheese over the phyllo with a spatula. Cover with plastic wrap and refrigerate for 1 hour, or until the cheese is firm.

6 Preheat the oven to 200 degrees F.

7 Lift the plastic wrap off the cheese-covered phyllo rec-tangle. Using a sharp knife, cut it into three 3 x 12-inch strips. Stack the strips, one on top of the other. Place the reserved plain strip on the top. Gently lifting each one with a spatula, transfer the napoléon to a baking sheet and warm in the oven for 1 minute.

8 Remove from the oven and cut crosswise into six 2 x 3-inch rectangles. Serve immediately.

▶ Do not put the napoléon together more than four hours before serving or the pastry will get soggy.

JEAN-GEORGES VONGERICHTEN: Napoléon of Roquefort and Boursin

Wild Mushroom Crêpes

SERVES 6
PREPARATION TIME: ABOUT 30 MINUTES
COOKING TIME: ABOUT 45 MINUTES
CHILLING TIME (CREPE BATTER ONLY): AT LEAST 20 MINUTES

Gâteau de Crêpes aux Champignons Sauvages

This is a basic crêpe recipe made special with mushrooms and a soy vinaigrette. Any type of wild mushrooms may be used.

6 tablespoons unsalted butter
1 shallot, chopped
1 clove garlic, chopped
4 ounces fresh porcini mushrooms, wiped clean, trimmed, and roughly chopped
4 ounces fresh shiitake mushrooms, wiped clean, trimmed, and roughly chopped
4 ounces fresh button mushrooms, wiped clean, trimmed, and roughly chopped
Salt and freshly ground black pepper to taste
1 tablespoon minced fresh chervil
1 tablespoon minced fresh chives
1 cup all-purpose flour
3 large eggs
1 cup milk
¼ cup soy sauce
¼ cup fresh lemon juice
1 cup olive oil

1 Assemble the *mise en place* trays for this recipe (see page 9).

2 In a medium-sized sauté pan, melt 2 tablespoons of the butter over medium-high heat. Add the shallot and garlic and sauté for about 3 minutes, until translucent.

3 Stir in the mushrooms and season to taste with salt and pepper. Reduce the heat and sauté for about 5 minutes, or until all the liquid from the mushrooms has evaporated.

4 Transfer the mushrooms to a blender or a food processor fitted with the metal blade. Process, using on/off turns, until finely chopped. Scrape the mushrooms into a bowl and stir in the chervil and chives. Set aside.

5 In a small saucepan, melt the remaining 4 tablespoons of butter over medium heat. Heat for about 3 minutes, or until golden brown. Take care the butter does not burn. Remove from the heat.

JEAN-GEORGES VONGERICHTEN: **Wild Mushroom Crêpes**

6 In a bowl, whisk together the flour, eggs, milk, and salt to taste until smooth. Whisk in browned butter. Cover and refrigerate for 20 minutes.

7 Preheat the oven to 400 degrees F.

8 To make the crêpes, heat a 6- or 7-inch nonstick crêpe pan over medium heat. Pour in just enough batter (about 2 tablespoons) to cover the bottom of the pan. Cook for 1 minute, or until light brown on the bottom and set. Carefully turn the crêpe and cook the other side for about 1 minute, or just until golden. Lift the crêpe from the pan and lay on a sheet of wax paper. Continue making the crêpes until you have made 8, stacking one on top of the other as you go. Use any leftover batter to make extra crêpes and freeze them for another use.

9 Lay the crêpes out on a work surface. Spread an equal portion of mushrooms evenly over the top of 7 of the crêpes.

10 Neatly stack the mushroom-topped crêpes, one on top of the other on a small non-stick baking sheet. Place the plain crêpe on top. Bake for about 10 minutes, until the top crêpe is lightly browned.

11 Meanwhile, in a bowl, whisk together the soy sauce and lemon juice. Whisk in the olive oil.

12 Remove the crêpe stack from the oven and cut into 6 wedges.

13 Ladle 2 to 3 tablespoons of the soy vinaigrette into the centers of 6 warm plates. Place a wedge of crêpe on each plate and serve immediately.

▶ You may have a little more soy vinaigrette than you need for this recipe. Store, covered and refrigerated, for up to a week. Use as dressing for meat, poultry or salads.

▶ When serving the vinaigrette as a garnish, as in this recipe, do not overmix: You want the soy to "bead" out of the oil (form little droplets).

▶ If you want to make the crêpes ahead of time and store them in the refrigerator, stack them between sheets of waxed paper. (This will make them easier to separate.) There is no need to bring them to room temperature before spreading the mushroom mixture on them.

▶ If you make extra crêpes, stack them between sheets of waxed paper, wrap the stack in a double thickness of plastic, and freeze for up to 1 month.

Beet Tartare

SERVES 6
PREPARATION TIME: ABOUT 25 MINUTES
COOKING TIME: ABOUT 1 HOUR
CHILLING TIME: 30 MINUTES

Tartare de Betteraves Rouges

Chef Vongerichten got this idea from steak tartare. In his bistro restaurant, JoJo, he sometimes serves the beet tartare topped with a sautéed sea scallop. He has also used golden beets, which taste very good, but the "beef" tartare symbolism doesn't work without the deep red beets!

1 pound beets, trimmed, washed, and quartered
1 shallot, chopped
2 teaspoons chopped cornichons
2 teaspoons chopped capers
2 teaspoons chopped fresh parsley
1 teaspoon mayonnaise
Salt and freshly ground black pepper to taste
Tabasco to taste
1 teaspoon sherry wine vinegar
3 tablespoons extra-virgin olive oil

1 Preheat the oven to 300 degrees F. Assemble the *mise en place* trays for this recipe (see page 9).

2 Spread the beets in a shallow baking dish. Add enough water to come ½ inch up the sides of the pan. Cover tightly with aluminum foil and roast for 1 hour. Remove the foil and cool the beets in their cooking juices.

3 Peel the beets, reserving the cooking juices. Put the beets in a blender or a food processor fitted with the metal blade, and process until just chopped.

4 Transfer the beets to a bowl. Stir in the shallot, cornichons, capers, parsley, and mayonnaise. Season to taste with salt, pepper, and Tabasco. Cover and refrigerate for at least 30 minutes.

5 Using a soup spoon, scoop out a heaping mound of

beets. Use a second spoon to form the mound into a quenelle (a rounded oval). Set a quenelle in the center of each of 6 serving plates. Let the quenelles come to room temperature.

6 In a bowl, whisk together the reserved beet-cooking juices, the vinegar, and olive oil. Season to taste with salt and pepper. Drizzle in a circle around the edge of the beet quenelles and serve.

▶ Do not chop the ingredients too fine or you will lose the juices.

▶ Do not serve ice-cold. The flavor is better at room temperature.

▶ You can form the quenelles without refrigerating the beet mixture, but it is easier if the mixture is cold. You can also form the quenelles with your hands. Dampen your hands first with cold water to keep the beets from sticking.

JEAN-GEORGES VONGERICHTEN:
Beet Tartare

Passion Fruit Club with Strawberries

"Club" de Fruits de la Passion aux Fraises

These represent an innovative French chef's exploration of a favorite American sandwich. The exotic flavor of the passion fruit gives an arresting taste to the pastry cream.

COOKIE TRIANGLES:
4 cups all-purpose flour
¾ cup granulated sugar
1 cup unsalted butter
1 teaspoon pure vanilla extract
2 large eggs
2 tablespoons water

PASSION FRUIT FILLING:
¾ cup milk
⅔ cup passion fruit purée (see note)
1 vanilla bean, split
⅓ cup granulated sugar
2 tablespoons all-purpose flour
1 large egg
2 tablespoons heavy cream, softly whipped
18 strawberries, washed, hulled, and halved lengthwise
3 tablespoons confectioners' sugar

1 Assemble the *mise en place* trays for this recipe (see page 9).

2 To make the cookies, in a bowl, combine the flour and sugar. Using two kitchen knives, cut in the butter until the mixture resembles coarse meal.

3 In a small bowl, whisk together the vanilla, eggs, and water. Add to the flour mixture and stir to make a stiff dough. Form into a ball, wrap in plastic, and allow to rest for 1 hour at room temperature.

4 Preheat the oven to 350 degrees F. Make a cardboard triangle pattern that is 1½ inches long from apex to base.

5 On a lightly floured surface, roll out the dough to a large circle about ⅛ inch thick.

6 Lay the cardboard pattern on the dough and, using a small sharp knife, cut out 20 or more triangles. (You will

◁ JEAN-GEORGES VONGERICHTEN: **Passion Fruit Club with Strawberries**

need only 18 but make extra to allow for breakage.) Transfer the triangles to an ungreased baking sheet. Bake for about 10 minutes, until very lightly browned. Remove from the oven, lift from the pan, and cool on a wire rack.

7 To make the passion fruit filling, in a medium-sized, heavy-based saucepan, combine the milk, passion fruit purée, and vanilla bean. Bring to a boil over medium heat. Remove from heat.

8 In a medium-sized bowl, whisk together the sugar, flour, and egg. Slowly whisk in the hot milk mixture and then return the mixture to the saucepan. Place over medium heat and bring to a boil, whisking continuously. Reduce the heat and cook, whisking continuously, for about 5 minutes until thick. Remove from the heat and allow to cool.

9 Remove the vanilla bean from the cooled pastry cream. Fold in the whipped cream.

10 On a work surface, lay out 6 of the cookie triangles. Place a strawberry half in each corner. Spoon a little passion fruit pastry cream into the center. Top each one with another cookie and repeat the layer with strawberries and pastry cream. Top with the remaining cookies and serve immediately.

Note: Passion fruit purée can be difficult to find. Try ordering it from a specialty store or buy some from a local restaurant. (It is easily available to restaurants through wholesalers.) If you cannot find passion fruit purée, substitute peach purée.

▶ If the strawberries are large, you may have to quarter them. In that case, you will need only 9 berries.

▶ To make passion fruit purée yourself, purée the flesh of 12 passion fruits in a food processor fitted with the metal blade. Strain the purée into a nonreactive saucepan and add ½ cup of sugar. Cook, stirring, over medium heat until the sugar dissolves. Increase the heat and bring to a boil. Immediately take the purée from the heat and strain again. Let it cool to room temperature and use it as instructed, or refrigerate it until needed.

Glossary

Al dente: Italian term meaning, literally, "to the tooth." Most often used to describe pasta that has been cooked until it is just tender but still offers some resistance to the tooth when chewed. Can also be used to describe the degree to which certain vegetables should be cooked.

Bard: To tie fat around lean meats, poultry, or game to keep the meat moist during roasting. The fat is removed just before the end of cooking, to allow browning.

Blanc: A liquid preparation used to cook light-colored and certain other vegetables or white offal, to keep them from discoloring. It is usually a mixture of water, lemon juice or vinegar, and flour. Seasoning may be added.

Bouquet garni: A combination of herbs either tied together or wrapped in a cheesecloth bag and used to flavor sauces, stews, soups, and stocks. The classic French combination is parsley, thyme, and bay leaf.

Caramelize: To heat sugar until it becomes syrupy and turns a rich golden to dark brown.

Chiffonade: A preparation of greens, classically sorrel, chicory, or lettuce, cut into strips of varying degrees of thickness. Easily done by rolling the leaves up cigar fashion and slicing crosswise. Used as a garnish for soups and cold hors d'oeuvres.

Chinois: A conical strainer with a handle, usually having an extremely fine mesh. Used to strain liquids that must be exceptionally smooth, often by pushing on the solids with a pointed wooden pestle.

Clarified butter: Butter that has been heated and skimmed so that all the milk solids are removed, leaving only the clear yellow fat. See page 12 for instructions for clarifying butter.

Cornichon: An imported French gherkin made from tiny pickled cucumbers. Very sour and crisp. Often used as a garnish for pâtés or smoked meats.

Deglaze: To add a liquid, usually wine or stock, to the cooking juices and sediment stuck to the bottom of a pan after sautéeing or roasting meats or vegetables. This is heated and the resulting liquid is often used as a base for a sauce to be served with the ingredients cooked in the pan.

Duxelles: A mixture of finely chopped mushrooms, onions, and shallots sautéed in butter until almost paste-like. Herbs can be added for additional flavor. Used as a stuffing or garnish.

Guinea hen: A small game bird, a relative of the partridge, thought to have originated in West Africa. Its somewhat gamey, lean, dry meat is usually barded or casseroled to keep it moist.

Julienne: Refers to foods, particularly vegetables, that have been cut into uniform thin strips, usually about the size of a matchstick. The vegetable to be julienned is first cut into slices of uniform thickness and then the slices are stacked and cut into even strips. Classically, these strips are 1 inch long by ¼ inch thick. Usually used as a decorative garnish. See page 12 for instructions on making julienne.

Lemon verbena: A potent, slender-leaf herb with a strong lemon flavor. Often used to flavor drinks and sweet and cold dishes.

Lovage: A large celery-like plant whose leaves, stalks, and seeds are used to flavor foods. The seeds are often just called celery seeds. Called *céleri bâtard* (false celery) in France. Also known as smellage.

Mandoline: A stainless-steel vegetable slicer composed of a folding stand and two blades. Used to cut vegetables into uniform slices or matchsticks.

Mesclun: A mixture of very young shoots and leaves of wild plants used for salads. Mesclun also can contain baby lettuces and leafy herbs.

Mince: To chop very fine.

Mortar: A round, concave container, often made of marble, porcelain, or wood, used to hold foods that are to be hand-ground using a pestle.

Paupiette: A thin slice of meat or fowl covered with a seasoned mixture of meat or vegetables and rolled up and tied. Often covered with a barding of bacon. Usually braised in stock or wine.

Pestle: A utensil used to pound food in a mortar. It can be rounded or pointed depending on the mortar. It is usually made of the same material as the mortar.

Poach: To cook food by gently simmering in seasoned liquid.

Quenelle: Traditionally, a light dumpling made of seasoned meat, fish, or poultry, molded into a small oval and poached. Also used to describe the oval shape.

Quince: A large, yellow, fall fruit with dry, astringent flesh that tastes like a cross between a pear and an apple. It is always eaten cooked.

Saffron: An intensely aromatic spice from the dried stigmas of a small crocus. It is the world's most costly spice, as it takes about 70,000 stigmas to make one pound. It is an integral part of many Mediterranean dishes, imparting a yellow-orange color and a somewhat bitter flavor to paella, bouillabaisse, and risotto milanese, among other foods.

Sear: To brown meat or poultry by cooking over (or under) intense heat. This process is used to seal in the juices before longer cooking.

Terrine: A deep, ovenproof dish with slanted sides, handles and a tight-fitting lid. The preparations made in the dish are also called terrines. They may be made from meats, poultry, fish, or vegetables, and are usually highly seasoned and often covered in gelatin or fat.

Tourner: Usually, to trim vegetables into uniform oval shapes, classically with 7 sides, using a small knife. *Tourner* has a number of other French culinary meanings as well, including the folding of croissant dough (see Techniques, page 12).

Truss: To hold meat or poultry in a compact shape by sewing it with a trussing needle threaded with kitchen twine or by tying the meat or poultry with kitchen twine.

Index

CONVERSION CHART

WEIGHTS AND MEASURES

1 teaspoon = 5 milliliters
1 tablespoon = 3 teaspoons = 15 milliliters
1/8 cup = 2 tablespoons = 1 fluid ounce = 30 milliliters
1/4 cup = 4 tablespoons = 2 fluid ounces = 59 milliliters
1/2 cup = 8 tablespoons = 4 fluid ounces = 118 milliliters
1 cup = 16 tablespoons = 8 fluid ounces = 237 milliliters
1 pint = 2 cups = 16 fluid ounces = 473 milliliters
1 quart = 4 cups = 32 fluid ounces = 946 milliliters (.96 liter)
1 gallon = 4 quarts = 16 cups = 128 fluid ounces = 3.78 liters

1 ounce = 28 grams
1/4 pound = 4 ounces = 114 grams
1 pound = 16 ounces = 454 grams
2.2 pounds = 1,000 grams = 1 kilogram